*Policy Bureaucracy*

# Policy Bureaucracy

## Government with a cast of thousands

Edward C Page and Bill Jenkins

# OXFORD

UNIVERSITY PRESS

Great Clarendon Street, Oxford OX2 6DP

Oxford University Press is a department of the University of Oxford.
It furthers the University's objective of excellence in research, scholarship,
and education by publishing worldwide in

Oxford New York

Auckland Cape Town Dar es Salaam Hong Kong Karachi
Kuala Lumpur Madrid Melbourne Mexico City Nairobi
New Delhi Shanghai Taipei Toronto

With offices in

Argentina Austria Brazil Chile Czech Republic France Greece
Guatemala Hungary Italy Japan Poland Portugal Singapore
South Korea Switzerland Thailand Turkey Ukraine Vietnam

Oxford is a registered trade mark of Oxford University Press
in the UK and in certain other countries

Published in the United States
by Oxford University Press Inc., New York

British Library Cataloguing in Publication Data
Data available

Library of Congress Cataloging in Publication Data
Data available

Typeset by SPI Publisher Services, Pondicherry, India
Printed in Great Britain
on acid-free paper by
Biddles Ltd.
King's Lynn, Norfolk

ISBN 0-19-928041X   978-0-19-928041-4

1 3 5 7 9 10 8 6 4 2

# Preface

'Actually, childbirth got quite stressful', said the tall, slim man in his thirties, dressed in a smart grey suit, 'it was just me and I was given all this responsibility'. He was referring to a job he had looking after a particular aspect of health care policy rather than any physiological miracle. Policymaking is often assumed to involve activism, advocacy, and asserting preferences in the cut and thrust of politics. Yet it also brings with it the active participation of people whose main connection with the policy in question owes little to any normative, still less emotional, attachment to the issue. Many people are involved in policymaking because particular policy responsibilities have been assigned to them as part of their bureaucratic jobs. Such people may be, in fact almost invariably are, extremely interested in their work, and are able to take great pride in what they achieve and to bring professionalism and enthusiasm to it. But they are simply not policy activists, and neither would one want them to be.

Policymaking is in part a political process, but it is also a bureaucratic one. Long before laws are drafted, policy commitments made, or groups consulted on government proposals, officials will have been working away to shape the policy in a form in which it can be presented to ministers and the world outside. Policy bureaucracies, parts of government organizations with specific responsibility for maintaining and developing policy, have to be mobilized before most significant policy initiatives are launched—although, as we will see, they may also be mobilized to make sense of policy initiatives after they have been announced by politicians. The key players in policy bureaucracies are not the top civil servants alone, the ones we know most about, such as permanent secretaries. In policy bureaucracies responsibility for maintaining and developing a specific area of policy rests to a large extent on middle-ranking officials, and our study concentrates on their role within policy bureaucracies. Such officials are not only present in the room when major policy issues are being decided—during the bilateral meetings between spending ministries and the Treasury when budgets are being negotiated or in the private offices of Secretaries of State and junior ministers—but they are also active participants in what is going on. Our study includes officials who helped originate policies that were subsequently taken over as manifesto commitments by the Labour Party, who helped devise the formula by which billions of pounds are allocated to local government in grants, and who recommended to a secretary of State that a controversial publisher should be allowed to take over a national newspaper.

Policy bureaucracies are not simply subordinate organizations that merely do as they are told by their political masters. They cannot be, as the main part of their work is to create solutions to problems; if politicians knew how they wanted the problems solved sufficiently to give their administrative subordinates direct instructions, they would not need policy bureaucracies. Politicians are often not even generally aware that such policy problems exist before their policy officials raise them. To work on the assumption that policymaking starts off with the top brass—ministers, permanent secretaries, and the like—setting out the broad direction, and all that is left to those below them is to fill in the details in a routine or mechanical way is plain wrong. It is not wrong because such officials 'act above their pay grade' in the words of Alastair Campbell, the Prime Minister's Head of Communications at the time of the Hutton Inquiry in Autumn 2003,[1] implying that officials may seek to have greater influence than their position suggests they should have. They may sometimes be presumptuous in this way. Yet it is not the point of this book to find and describe examples of officials having such *folie de grandeur*, and we must admit to not finding any particularly clear cases where they did. We might have expected to find such instances, and should have been disappointed that we did not, if we had paid too much attention to much of the recent theoretical literature on bureaucracy that seeks to understand the motivations of politicians and bureaucrats by assuming an inherent power conflict between them (Huber and Shipan 2002; see Goodsell 2004 for a critical view). Officials are acting *within* their pay grade when they are involved in shaping policy. Indeed, doing 'policy work' is a conventional term used by officials in the UK to describe a certain range of jobs that middle-ranking as well as senior officials do. We simply do not know what middle-ranking officials do when they are acting within their pay grade. How such middle-ranking officials in policy bureaucracies are involved in policy-making as part of their everyday jobs is the central question of this book.

We first approached this issue in a spirit of curiosity, wanting to find out about a group of officials, and a type of work, about which little was known, and used an approach that might be described as barefoot empiricism, since we set out with the simple methodology of asking the people concerned to talk about themselves—an approach discussed further below. However, it gradually struck us that the questions we were asking and the answers we were starting to explore had somewhat wider theoretical resonances. The relationship between leaders and their subordinates is one of the key questions of organizational sociology. Organizational sociology looks at diverse organizations including employment agencies and factories. When the organization happens to be a ministerial bureaucracy, the relationship takes on an additional dimension. Leadership is not only about getting things done; it is also about the character of democracy. The particular challenge to leadership in a democracy raised by our middle-ranking officials was that posed by specialization and expertise in bureaucratic organizations in general and 'staff' organizations (i.e. concerned with strategic decision-making issues rather than the 'line' tasks of managing personnel and delivery) in particular: baldly stated, how is it possible to control or give direction to the work of people who know more about the particular subject in hand than the people supposed to be in charge?

This question brought us directly back into the territory of Weber (1988) and the conflict between hierarchy and expertise within Weber's theory of bureaucracy that is at the heart of

Gouldner's *Patterns of Industrial Bureaucracy* (1954). We claim to apply neither Weber nor Gouldner, but rather use them to help structure our questions, our answers, and our discussion of the implications of our answers. They steered our analysis with a light touch, but we could not possibly have made sense of our material without them. One substantial drawback from locating our discussion within classical bureaucratic theory is that the term 'bureaucracy' has, outside social science, negative associations with, among other things, red tape, slowness, pettifoggery, and unnecessarily convoluted procedures. Our empirical research found no substantial evidence of such negative features in the world of Whitehall. Our results suggest quite the reverse—policy officials are able to work fast, flexibly, and with a clear sense of proportion. Yet abandoning the term 'bureaucracy' simply to avoid a popular distortion of its more scientific meaning was too high a price to pay, since it would have made development of the theoretical approach we wanted to use awkward, if not impossible.

Our approach to our subject does not start with a set of theoretically based hypotheses. When so little is known about a group, such as middle-ranking officials, and how it works, description and understanding come before theoretical explanation. Here we take our cue from Crozier's *Bureaucratic Phenomenon* (1964) and his 'clinical method', which, in a nutshell, is largely inductive since it

bears on particular cases, and generalises only from an intimate understanding of these cases. . . . [It] can serve us better than a systematic approach that seeks immediately to establish rigorous laws and thus gives the impression of being more scientific.   (Crozier 1964: 4)

Crozier eschews the 'affirmation of banal interdependencies' through sociological laws in favour of '*examples* of models of systems of relations in action . . . [which] can teach us more about the functioning of the social systems on the same order and even much larger systems than laws which a premature rigor has kept from being adequately comprehensive' (Crozier 1964: 4–5). Crozier's 'clinical method' aims to produce valid generalization precisely by not taking such generalization or assumptions of

relationships between component parts as a starting point. Rather, theoretical generalization is the finishing point.

We have largely avoided direct discussion of other more currently fashionable theoretical perspectives such as principal–
agent theory, neo-institutionalism, network/'policy community'
frameworks, or broader rational choice approaches, which lay
claim to being 'at the heart of much of the modern "scholarship" '
in the 'modern scientific study of bureaucracy' (Krause and Meier
2003: 7). We expect to be criticized for this gap and we have to
admit that such approaches, in the hands of others, might con-
ceivably have done a creditable job. We had three reasons for not
using such approaches. First, since part of our aim was to give an
understandable picture of one particular slice of life, the working
life of relatively junior officials in a policy bureaucracy, too much
theoretical clutter and jargon would stand in the way of a clear
portrayal of sets of activities that can be described and understood
in fairly straightforward terms. Second, while we have no doubt
that interesting questions about middle-ranking officials can be
framed in the language of such theories, we also have no doubt
that choosing one of them is likely to shut out at least as many
important questions as it sought to address. Third, such theories
struck us as rather limited, since with respect to public bureaucracies they often satisfy themselves with theoretical explanations of
empirical phenomena that are already well understood through
other mechanisms, including common sense. Despite the passing
of six decades and a massive expansion in the number of people
studying public administration and policymaking in the UK, in
our view the most sophisticated insights into civil service activity
below the very top level are to be found in Kingsley's *Representative
Bureaucracy* (1944).

Kingsley's book now sadly has the status of a classic only by
virtue of being widely misquoted. It is usually cited as an early
statement of the principle that the presence of officials from
diverse social groups in a bureaucracy allows such groups to be
represented in a political sense in bureaucratic decision-making
(e.g. Sowa and Selden 2003). Yet he was arguing almost the exact

opposite. The pre-war UK civil service in its composition and operation replicated, he argued, wider patterns of class stratification, and top decision-making positions were overwhelmingly occupied by people from the upper middle class. As a bureaucracy the UK system was 'representative' since 'Ministers and Civil Servants share the same backgrounds and hold similar social views' (Kingsley 1944: 273). Using this central insight, Kingsley offers a rich analysis of the pre-war UK civil service that goes beyond a narrow focus on the top. Kingsley's work also provides a firm link between Gouldner's examination of an upstate New York gypsum mine in the early 1950s and a study of middle-level Whitehall officials. Gouldner (1954: 204) cites Kingsley's book as the source of the name given to the distinctive form of 'representative bureaucracy' he contrasts with the more traditional 'punishment-centred' version.

The way we chose to examine how middle-ranking officials in policy bureaucracies work was to speak to the civil servants themselves. The methodology and selection of officials for analysis is covered in the Appendix. Although this research relies upon the perceptions and understandings of large numbers of individuals, it is conducted through observation of the organization in action and does not seek systematically to measure them through survey research. The Cabinet Office, despite folklore to the contrary, agreed that a factual survey of middle-ranking officials using a sensitively framed instrument might be possible (see also Kuper and Marmot 2003 for examples of large civil service surveys by self-administered questionnaires). We might have expected such a survey at the very least to have allowed us to have greater confidence in the degree to which our statements about how civil servants work applied across the civil service. Gouldner (1954: 17–18) succinctly sets out the nature of the methodological choice in such circumstances by quoting from the sociologist, George Homans:

Sociology may miss a great deal if it tries to be too quantitative too soon. Data are not nobler because they are quantitative.... Lord Nelson, greatest of all admirals, after explaining to his ship captains the plan of attack he intended to use at the battle of Trafalgar, went on to say, 'No Captain can do very wrong who places his ship alongside that of an enemy'. In the same way, no one who studies a group will go far wrong if he gets close to it, and by whatever methods are available, observes all that he can. . . . The statistician may find fault with the passages for not letting him know the relation between the 'sample' and the 'universe'. . . . His criticisms are good, and they can only be answered by raising new questions: How much more effort, in men, time and money, would be needed to get the kind of data he wants? Given a limited supply of all three . . . [t]hese are questions not of scientific morality but of strategy.

We decided against a survey at an early stage. We had never been sure that a survey would be a *sine qua non* for the study, and we started our interviews with the intention of seeing how far we could go with interviews alone before developing firm plans for a survey and securing the necessary permission. In the course of the interviews, we encountered all sorts of potential technical problems with a survey of this group of civil servants, not least the problem of devising a sampling frame for any random selection of respondents. Central lists of those in the relevant grades do not exist in a form accessible to an outside researcher.

Another important reason for deciding not to try to conduct a survey was that the more we interviewed, the more we realized that the most informative and illuminating responses were to questions that were highly context-specific. General questions about the roles that civil servants thought they filled or how civil servants get on with ministers never offered the immediacy or clarity of response we got to questions about what the person sitting in front of us had been doing today or what happened to him or her the last time he or she had to deal with the minister. Our questions probed how officials went about *doing* their jobs, rather than what they *thought* about abstract or hypothetical propositions of the sort that tend to be found in self-administered questionnaires or interviewer-administered survey instruments. Our methodology again brought us closer to Gouldner's *Patterns of Industrial Bureaucracy* (1954) than, say, *Bureaucrats and Politicians in Western Democracies* by Aberbach et al. (1981).

*4*

In addition, we did not have the resources for an elaborate interviewer-administered survey, which would have brought with it problems of access. In short, the real choice we faced as researchers was not whether to use short interviews or a longer questionnaire, but whether we used the short interviews (see Appendix) or nothing at all. The methodological question then becomes whether our approach would be able to throw sufficient light on the issue of how a policy bureaucracy works, to make it worthwhile. We believe it does, but must leave others to decide.

Our methodology thus relies upon middle-ranking officials' reports of how they do their work as provided by interviews as well as the published material and information available from other sources (including academic literature, practitioner publications, and Internet sources). The interviews, of which we conducted 128 with middle-ranking officials, asked what officials were doing at the moment and probed how they went about their tasks. From the interviews and printed material we were able to build up a good picture of the range of policy work involving officials at this level and provide not only a descriptive account of what they do but also some answers to the central questions about how officials in Whitehall staff positions manage their subordination and their policymaking activities. Our access to officials was predominantly at this middle-ranking level. While it may be a gap in our analysis that we were only able to look at elite perspectives to a limited extent, we have coped with this gap by trying to be cautious in our interpretation of the story we were hearing from the middle-ranking officials we interviewed. To identify possible biases is not to deal with them. In our conclusions we try to briefly explore whether and how our results might have been biased by our method. But we believe that the policy-work of those in the middle ranks is sufficiently important to justify the focus on them. In time we would like permission to go back and cover the role of senior officials in the policy process, but realize that to gain permission to draw on an even more substantial amount of officials' time, we need to demonstrate that we can make something of what we have already got.

One of the acknowledged problems of research that relies heavily on interviews is that of how much trust to place in what the interviewer is told. It is less a problem that respondents tell untruths and more that the interview asks respondents not only to reflect on what they do but also share their reflections with a complete stranger, and an outsider too. This brings all sorts of possible biases including the possibility that respondents will slant their comments to what they think the interviewer wants to hear, will be reticent on matters that could cause them trouble or embarrassment if what they had said were widely known, or that they will simply exaggerate their role in any process they describe.

These three sources of bias have almost certainly come up in our interviews. The trouble is we have no knowledge of which ones they came up in. We did not see it as our job to check on the veracity of responses. Where available, documentary evidence in the form of government documents (published and unpublished) and newspapers was used in conjunction with our interviews. Cross-reference with existing documentation was not used to try and ascertain that we had been told the truth, but rather to fill in the background to what we had been told and save time in interviews to ask about things for which there was no written record. To have sought extra interviews with the object of checking up on people one had already spoken to—and it would have been impossible to ask the right questions without it being obvious one was checking up on a colleague interviewed previously—would probably have resulted in us being shown the door. Interviews like those in this book cannot be conducted in a context of low trust. Our approach throughout is not that our interviews have shown us the 'true' picture, but rather that we present an honest picture based on what our interviews tell us, and we present a reasonable amount of evidence to substantiate any claims we make. We were critical of the value of some of our interview material—comments made as a joke, or where we hit on a raw nerve or a sensitive issue, or, more often, answers offered in polite response to an ambiguous or poorly conceived question. Yet we think it best to leave the plain and unblemished truth to evangelists and concentrate on being honest to the best of our abilities.

This study is based on interviewing middle-ranking officials. It does not deal directly with the people with whom they interact—including junior and senior civil servants, ministers, interest groups, parliamentarians (both government and opposition), and judicial authorities. Middle-ranking officials occupy a role in the centre of the stage in policy bureaucracies. This is not to prejudge the issue that they are important in shaping policy outcomes, but in many key issues they happen to be at least in close contact with all the known major players in almost all significant policy decisions (a point elaborated on in Chapter 4). As researchers on a limited budget we faced a methodological choice between breadth and depth of coverage. A deeper coverage would allow us to assess the precise role of the middle-ranking official in any handful of policy issues. We chose breadth of coverage since it allows us to say something about the character of middle-ranking officials as a group rather than about the limited number of officials who happened to be involved in at most a handful of policies. In addition to their socio-demographic characteristics we can look at the range of tasks they fill, how they perceive their jobs, how they go about doing them, and their relations with other key players. All these things are viewed almost exclusively from the perspective of the officials concerned. Many of the episodes and issues to which respondents refer are documented, and as already suggested, this allows for the introduction of other perspectives. But this book offers an account of the policy process in the UK as viewed from the vantage point of the middle-ranking official.

Confession may be good for the soul but not for the mind. Recognizing that the methodology of this study could be offering a biased perspective only starts to have any scientific meaning if one can explore and evaluate how a different methodology might have produced a different set of results. We attempt to do this in our conclusion.

In the drafts of this book, penned before the research on it had been completed, we included a passage to the effect that middle-ranking officials were generally a neglected group. In the academic literature on public policy this remains true. Carpenter's historical study (2001) highlights the role of the 'mezzo' level of bureaucracy in creating support for government agencies, although his definition includes officials senior to those used in our analysis. It is possible to find the odd passage alluding to the influence of middle-ranking officials—aside from Kingsley (1944). Kellner and Crowther-Hunt (1980: 153–8) highlight the role of the Principal (Grade 7 in more recent terminology) in helping shape policy. Scott (1999: 52) writes: 'In modern democracies, protection of people's liberties from arbitrary exercise of official authority requires as much, or more, attention to the pedestrian activities of minor officials than to the majestic proceedings of Parliament or Congress'; and Weiler (1999) points out the importance of domestic and international civil servants below the top grades in the European Union context. Such observations are rare and usually unaccompanied by much empirical evidence on how such officials shape policy. When we started the research, middle-ranking officials were also generally unlikely to feature in newspaper headlines apart from vague occasional references to 'officials' deciding this or that.

In 2003 and 2004 middle-ranking officials contrived to hit the headlines more often than in the past. In 2004 a Home Office minister, Beverley Hughes, resigned following an immigration scandal about which she had claimed that her officials had not kept her properly informed ('Explained: the Hughes affair', *The Guardian*, 1 April 2004). Bettina Crossick, a seconded official from the Probation Service, a Grade 7 post,[2] hit the headlines when the details of the arrangements made to resettle and protect Maxine Carr after her release from prison were stolen from her car. Carr had given a false alibi for a double child murderer in a high-profile trial. Crossick was described as a 'top adviser'—'such is her seniority', one leading broadsheet newspaper wrote ('The woman entrusted with fixing the new identity', *Daily Telegraph*, 15 May 2004), 'that it is believed she would have had direct contact with David Blunkett, briefing the Home Secretary...'. In other incidents the Secretary of State for Defence, Geoff Hoon, used the excuse that his civil servants had not passed on crucial documents for him to read. It became a standard subject for satire. For example, *Private Eye* (1106, 14 May 2004, p. 10) reported—when the television series *Dr Who* was scheduled to reappear on BBC—that 'Dr Hoon the Waste-of-Timelord returns in a new adventure in which he fails to read a Red Cross Report about Iraq. Repeating his favourite catchphrase "I knew nothing about it", Dr Hoon escapes in the Tardis and lives to fight another day'.

The interview research for this book was largely completed well before the case of one particular middle-ranking civil servant, David Kelly, hit the headlines. Half of it was in draft before he became a household name. Kelly had briefed journalists about the UK government's handling of intelligence information about Saddam Hussein's possession of, and capacity to deploy, 'weapons of mass destruction'. These briefings were used in news reports critical of the government's approach to Iraq and provoked visible anger among ministers, the Prime Minister, and his adviser, Alastair Campbell. Kelly's suicide gave rise to a judicial inquiry that dominated headlines for four months after it started its work in August 2003 and again when it produced its report in January 2004. That the government described him as a 'middle-ranking' official was an important part of the story, since in the press and media coverage this description was widely viewed as an attempt, above all by the Prime Minister's close advisers, to convey the impression that Kelly would not be able to judge what went on at the very highest levels of government. A middle-ranking official, so the implication went, would not know much about how intelligence information was used (see 'Campbell plots his way out of Kelly crisis', *The Scotsman*, 25 July 2003). But the Hutton Inquiry, with its focus on establishing the role of the British Broadcasting Corporation and the government in the circumstances surrounding Kelly's death, did not concentrate much on the status of Kelly as a middle-ranking official (Hutton 2004). Moreover, the evidence presented to the Hutton Inquiry shone a sharp light into the workings of government, and raised in a rather stark manner the issues of how expertise and obedience might occasionally conflict and how inexpert politicians should handle the work of specialists. Yet it did so in the context of what might be considered a highly unusual set of circumstances—the use of intelligence in making a public case for taking the UK into a war opposed by many of its citizens and allies. Our study seeks to establish the roles that truly middle-ranking officials routinely, in the sense of 'usual' rather than 'dull', play in everyday policymaking in the UK.

We developed this project together, but Page did the interviews and drafted the chapters. Our academic creditors include Jack Hayward, Lord Norton of Louth (University of Hull), Philip Cowley, Jan-Hinrik Meyer-Sahling (University of Nottingham), Michael Barzelay, George Jones, Christian List, Martin Lodge, Richard Rawlings (London School of Economics—LSE), and Rod Rhodes (Australian National University) for advice in developing the research. Jack Hayward helped change the whole shape of the book by pointing out that our (second) working title for the project, *Patterns of Policymaking Bureaucracy*, following Gouldner (1954), offered much more intellectual promise than the original working title *Civil Servants at Work*. This line was pursued for a paper delivered to a staff seminar at the LSE, and we are grateful to colleagues from the LSE Department of Government for their encouragement and critical comments. The comparative dimension to this project was developed in preparation for Page's delivery of the Henry Bellmon Lecture at the University of Oklahoma in April 2004. We are grateful to Guy Peters (University of Pittsburgh) and Charles Goodsell (Virginia Polytechnic Institute) for their help in developing this aspect of the work, James Ortiz from the Department of the Interior, Ronald Moe of the Congressional Research Service for useful guidance, and to Jos Raadschelders, Larry Hill (both University of Oklahoma), and Harvey Tucker (Texas A&M University) for their comments on it. Colin Thain (University of Ulster) provided useful add-itional insights into the working of the Treasury that we have included with his permission. Gabbie Hayes (University of Hull) helped organize the interviews and her organizational expertise made the research and its analysis possible. Jack Hayward, Jos

Raadschelders, Jan-Hinrik Meyer-Sahling, and George Jones made valuable comments on drafts of this book.

We are grateful to a large number of public servants for their help in this enterprise. Officials at the Public and Commercial Services Union (PCS), above all Charles Cochrane, helped us develop a strategy for approaching civil servants for interview. That Sir Richard Wilson (now Lord Wilson) and his successor Sir Andrew Turnbull were content for us to carry out a large number of interviews across Whitehall shows the inaccuracy of the general assumption that Whitehall is a secretive place. Juliet Mountford, currently at the Home Office, and later Eleanor Goodison of the Centre for Management and Policy Studies in the Cabinet Office, were our points of contact and helped us steer our way through the sets of interviews. We are especially grateful to the 140 officials (including our 128 respondents in the relevant grades and 12 other officials) who agreed to be interviewed for this research. They must remain anonymous, and this research would have been impossible without them volunteering to give up their time to talk to us. The interviews varied greatly in length and topic but never in the grace, patience, and good humour of the respondents. Every single interview was enjoyable and we hope that all who spoke to us believe this book to be a fair account of their valuable work.

The details of the interviews are set out in the Appendix. The interviews were not recorded electronically but through notes written up as soon as possible after the interview. We sent specially marked-up copies of the draft manuscript to our respondents, each of whom was given a number code that could be used to locate his or her words. Respondents were invited to check the book and suggest any amendments. The effect of this was to change very little. No respondent asked for his or her words to be deleted. Some of those interviewed proposed minor alterations, but these were generally to increase clarity. Where we have quoted from our interviews, we occasionally made minor changes, including changing the specific circumstances or proper names mentioned, in such a way as to help preserve where necessary the anonymity of our respondents, but not to alter in any material way the point being made.

The research was conducted before the development of the Cabinet Office's 'Professional Skills for Government' initiative launched in late 2004. The initiative contained proposals aimed at a radical transformation of the careers of officials doing policy work, above all by creating incentives for nurturing and developing specialized skills among civil servants (see Cabinet Office 2004a). If this ambitious programme succeeds in generating a shift away from 'generalist' skills within the civil service, we will need to return to examine how such a change has transformed wider relations, above all patterns of authority and how it is exercised, since we believe that the character of their expertise shapes how middle-ranking officials interact with their political and administrative superiors.

Edward C. Page
Bill Jenkins

# Contents

# Glossary

| | |
|---|---|
| ARA | Assets Recovery Agency |
| BBC | British Broadcasting Corporation |
| BMA | British Medical Association |
| BSE | Bovine Spongiform Encephalopathy |
| CBI | Confederation of British Industry |
| CMPS | Centre for Management and Policy Studies |
| COREPER | Committee of Permanent Representatives |
| DCMS | Department for Culture, Media and Sport |
| DEFRA | Department for Environment, Food and Rural Affairs |
| DETR | Department of the Environment, Transport and the Regions |
| DfES | Department for Education and Skills |
| DoH | Department of Health |
| DPM | Deputy Prime Minister |
| DTI | Department for Trade and Industry |
| DWP | Department for Work and Pensions |
| ECHR | European Convention on Human Rights |
| ENA | *Ecole Nationale d'Administration* |
| EO | Executive Officer |
| EU | European Union |
| HEO | Higher Executive Officer |
| HEO(D) | Higher Executive Officer (Development) |
| HRA | Human Rights Act |
| MAFF | Ministry of Agriculture, Fisheries and Food |
| MIDIT | Means of Identifying and Developing Individual Talent |
| MoD | Ministry of Defence |
| NATO | North Atlantic Treaty Organization |
| NDPB | Non-Departmental Public Body |
| NHS | National Health Service |
| ODPM | Office of the Deputy Prime Minister |

PCA      Parliamentary Commissioner for Administration
PCS      Public and Commercial Services Union
PFI      Private Finance Initiative
PIU      Performance and Innovation Unit
PSA      Public Service Agreement
RIA      Regulatory Impact Assessment
SCS      Senior Civil Service
SEO      Senior Executive Officer
SEU      Social Exclusion Unit
TUC      Trades Union Congress

# Government with a Cast of Thousands

## Policy as a bureaucratic activity

Kingdon (1985: 165) likens policy activists to tanned beach bums with sun-bleached hair, waiting with their surfboards at the ready to 'ride the big wave' as it comes along. This glamorous image certainly seems appealing and is presented as part of an outstandingly vivid account of an intensely political process of policymaking. Ideas, issues, and events mingle to provide opportunities, or 'windows', for policy action that need to be identified and handled skilfully by anyone who wants to shape public policy. Shaping policy is about picking up your board and jumping in when the time is right, and deploying your skills to use the forces out there to your own advantage. An altogether different type of board is used in Weber's famous evocation (1988: 560) of political activity as 'the strong slow boring of hard boards with both passion and an eye for perspective'. Here Weber is emphasizing the sheer hard work that goes into politics. Giving leadership to the potentially stifling bureaucratic machine is also a vitally important component of executive politics in a democratic state. He argues that imagination and reaching out for the impossible are required for anyone seeking 'politics as a vocation', but such occasional 'heroism' has to be mingled with much longer periods of routine 'leadership'—steering the bureaucratic state—if disillusion is not to destroy a political career.

Our previous understanding of policymaking has tended to concentrate more on the surfing and less on the heavy carpentry. However, policymaking is not only a political activity—involving the cut and thrust of politics and the manoeuvring of different politicians, groups, and individuals to shape policy—but also a bureaucratic one. It takes hard work to shape a policy into a form that can be put to ministers and a wider audience and turned into a set of policy instruments in the form of a law, plan, budget, consultation document, or even statement of intent. Politicians need bureaucrats to develop and maintain policy, not simply for 'advice' on how to do it. Parts of government organizations, not always easily identified in organograms, specialize in developing and maintaining policy in the form of policy bureaucracies. How they work and how they help shape policy is almost *terra incognita* in political science and public administration.

This book looks at how policy bureaucracies work from the point of view of the people who do the overwhelming bulk of policy work within them—middle-ranking officials. One of the abiding clichés about how executive government works is that 'policy'—the broad strategic direction of government—is set by the top, whether politicians or civil servants, and the detailed elaboration of this policy is, to use a phrase coined in a different context, 'embellishment and detail' (Pulzer 1967: 98). The top deals with the broad issues, and the narrow gauge work is done lower down. While we would not seek to contradict this view entirely, there is prima facie evidence to challenge the assumption that a hierarchy in the importance of decisions coincides with organizational hierarchy. Many important strategic policy issues involve settling detail, many strategic policy decisions emerge from the work of those developing detail, and those working at this level have substantial discretion and influence in shaping policy in this sense (see Page 2003).

To emphasize the bureaucratic dimension in the policymaking process, our view of government has to include as significant players people from much lower grades than we might have expected if we relied on main sources that, like Wilson and Barker

(2003: 354) tend to concentrate on 'officials who, by virtue of their rank, can be assumed to have the opportunity for involvement in important policy issues'—the very top, and for Wilson and Barker this rank is the top three grades, of Whitehall officialdom.[3] To move outside the top grades and question the assumption that they are the only civil servants who matter in this way fundamentally challenges assumptions about the way policy is made and the degree to which it can be steered or controlled, since many existing approaches to the question are based on the assumption of small numbers. Descriptions of 'policy communities' typically emphasize their restricted membership (see Rhodes 1997: Chapter 2 for a review). The 'top' civil service in the UK (see Chapter 2) contains just under 4,000 people. It has often been assumed (cf. Heclo and Wildavsky 1974) that only a fraction of these people, only those in the higher echelons even of this top level, are involved in a significant way in making policy. Yet many officials several grades below the very top do 'policy work'. If we extend the groups we are interested in to include all the 4,000 and add to them the people who are the subject of this research—the four grades below the top Senior Civil Service (SCS) level—the size of the group rises to over 106,000. This group includes a large proportion of people in jobs that are by any definition remote from 'policy' work;[4] even so it suggests that the policymaking community inside government might not be confined to a couple of hundred of the very top people but rather contains thousands and possibly tens of thousands.

## A cast of thousands

'Not a lot of people know that' is a reasonable enough reaction to this observation. It might be an interesting observation that when we think of policymaking as a bureaucratic activity, we have to take account of the fact that large numbers of lower-level bureaucrats do much work that shapes policy. So what? Cecil B. DeMille famously added a 'cast of thousands' to his 1956 version of the film *The Ten Commandments*. He produced glorious spectacles but they did not, and could not, change the essential nature of the story. Why should it matter that policy is made with a civil service cast of thousands? It is possible that the civil servants we are interested in should simply be viewed as extras, with at best the odd walk-on part here and there. There are three main answers to the question 'so what?' we may give to justify the focus on middle-ranking civil servants and on understanding what they do.

The first concerns the completeness of our understanding of who shapes policy. The socio-economic and cultural backgrounds of civil servants and their ideologies and outlooks on life are often assumed to have an important influence on their behaviour (Aberbach et al. 1981). Yet our understanding of these features of the bureaucracy as a social or occupational group is based almost entirely on what we know about a small and narrow tranche of bureaucratic life sliced from the top. The social backgrounds of bureaucrats have been a significant theme of UK and comparative bureaucracy studies. That an Oxbridge background has been emphasized in characterizing the social origins of UK civil servants, and is taken to be its distinguishing characteristic in cross-national studies of the subject (Aberbach et al. 1981), illustrates the overwhelming importance attached to officials in the upper grades. The motivations of bureaucrats have been at the heart of classic and more recent public choice approaches to public administration and policy. Downs' (1967) categorization of officials according to their main motivations (climbers, conservers, zealots, advocates, and statesmen) refers to those of senior officials, while the self-interest of senior administrators that produces the dominant 'bureau-shaping' motivation among officials is Dunleavy's variant (1991) of this approach. Expertise within the civil service, whether in the UK or in other countries, is generally assessed by the universities attended by the senior figures at the top (Ridley 1968; Peters 2000). In most matters touching on the social characteristics of civil servants—including mobility (Page 1997), ideology (Hooghe 2001), and career paths (Barberis 1996)—nearly everything we know about the role of civil services in the political system, whether in the UK or elsewhere, is seen from the perspective of the permanent secretary (or senior officials) and his (the world of the top civil servant is still in all developed countries predominantly male) near-peers.

Yet, as we shall show, the policymaking roles of those outside this narrow tranche are substantial. In the light of their role in making policy, an understanding of the characteristics of middle-ranking civil servants is important at least for the sake of completeness. Those lower down in the bureaucracy have different characteristics from those at the top—indeed the distinctiveness of senior officials is generally taken for granted, as it is rare to see direct comparisons among different grades of the educational and social backgrounds of officials. Thus the observation that top civil servants are almost entirely university graduates suggests that many of those in lower grades are not. Other key characteristics of bureaucrats as a social and occupational group are likely to be different as one explores below the very top levels of the civil service (see Sheriff 1976). While the civil servant in the UK is famously regarded, especially in contrast to continental European officials, as a 'generalist', how far does this lack of 'specialization' extend downwards? What does 'expertise' or 'specialization' mean at this level—does it involve an awareness of the political environment of policymaking, often argued to be the key skill needed for top civil servants? What of the loyalties of civil servants? The department is often assumed to be the prime focus for organizational loyalties among civil servants, yet we do not know whether this departmental loyalty applies equally to a more mobile top civil service and a less mobile middle and lower civil service.

The second reason for looking at the role of rank-and-file officials working within policy bureaucracies is the light such an examination throws on the core question of how policy is made. A cast of thousands does not just add an extra cohort of people whose names have to go in the credits for the sake of completeness, it also adds a crucial dimension that has been largely neglected in the study of policymaking: hierarchy. This dimension alters the perspective since the concentration on an elite group produces the picture of a world that is remarkably two-dimensional, where the main distinction between groups and actors is institutional. There are people with different institutional affiliations—people who belong to different ministries and other government organizations or stakeholder and interest groups—pitched together in a relatively flat decision-making arena agreeing policies or battling out the differences between themselves (e.g. Heclo and Wildavsky, 1974). It is a world in which different proposals, perspectives, and positions come readily formed, as major actors (or groups of actors) try their luck in the bargaining game, such as the Treasury's plans to cut spending, and the spending departments' desire to increase it; or the agricultural and environmental branches within a ministry looking after their own constituencies; or the new emphasis on 'joined-up' government that attempts to create and develop inter- and intra-departmental and organizational linkages (e.g. in initiatives aimed at combatting social exclusion; see National Audit Office 2001a). Some relief, in the geographical sense, is offered by the fact that the institutional affiliations of individuals—whether the people and groups involved are from the cabinet, party politics, civil service, or interest groups; and whether they are big players or small fry—enjoy different status and authority in the policy process as some are assumed to be 'insiders' and others 'outsiders', and some groups and institutions more powerful than others.

However, considering policy as a bureaucratic activity introduces a hierarchical dimension and we are forced to ask a series of different questions about the decision-making process. The most obvious is: what is the division of labour involved in making decisions within policy bureaucracies? Working out an organization-wide or 'departmental' stance on a particular issue is not a departmental decision, in the sense it is decided by some form of single meeting of the top people in the department which then becomes the blueprint for handling and developing that issue. What are the stages involved in making such a departmental policy? What is the range of jobs involved and who does the work? What cues do those involved have and what routines do they observe when they help shape policy? The question of the division of labour in turn raises the further question of whether and by what mechanisms any form of political control can be exercised over policy bureaucracies by both bureaucratic superiors and, perhaps most important, politicians. Lipsky's 'street-level bureaucrats' (1980)—police officers, social workers, and public health inspectors among others—operate in locations physically remote from authority and are thus not directly exposed to their superiors and have substantial discretion in doing their jobs. Our rank-and-file policy bureaucrats are in some respects similar. The span of control of those who manage them can be extremely wide and does not usually allow them to exercise close scrutiny and direction of their subordinates. In this sense we may term our middle-ranking officials 'first-floor' bureaucrats.[5]

Against this charge that lower levels of bureaucracy have been ignored in social science, it might be argued that the study of public policy has indeed looked at the division of labour in the policy process (Pressman and Wildavsky, 1973; Parsons 1995; Thain and Wright 1995; Hill and Hupe 2002). However, academic studies that have highlighted the different activities involved in making policy tend to evoke a much more extended set of phenomena than the actual central decision-making process (Rhodes 1997; Richards and Smith 2002). These phenomena include activities at pre-decision stages (covering those that shape what issues emerge as public policy issues, how they reach the agenda, and how they are handled) as well as post-decision stages (including implementation and evaluation). While *senior* bureaucrats may additionally 'advise' policymakers, the predominant view in the policy literature, where the role of *middle-ranking* officials is even discussed, is that their role is limited to implementation. As Kingdon (1985: 3) puts it: 'Implementation is the major preoccupation of career bureaucrats. Most of them are administering existing programs, not concentrating on new agenda items. The power of bureaucrats is often manifested in that implementation activity.' Yet we will see that the decision-making process—the sets of activities that accompany decisions to change laws, budgets or other regulatory frameworks in order to achieve new or altered objectives (or in order to achieve established objectives in a different way)—itself comprises a series of distinct stages. However, we know little about what these stages are and how people handle them.

The third reason for looking at the middle level of the bureaucracy has to do with the character of administrative reform. A whole series of reform initiatives has made major assumptions about what goes on at the middle level, yet virtually without any evidence. The famous criticism of the Fulton Committee (1968) Report was that by seeking to place experts at the top of the civil service it was overlooking the fact that such expertise does not belong at the top of the civil service, but lower down (Kellner and Crowther-Hunt 1980). Yet, in many ways, this myopia or disinclination to engage with the real world of civil service organization and bureaucracy is characteristic of continued efforts to 'reform' or 'modernize'. In part, what we see here is a manifestation of the politics of paradox (Gray and Jenkins 2003), which while differing—somewhat depending on the political persuasion of recent governments—also reveals a number of striking similarities not least in administrative reform programmes that frequently rest on conflicting objectives and a poorly articulated grasp of the realities of administrative life 'below the salt' of top Whitehall tables.

As part of the Modernising Government reforms, the Performance and Innovation Unit (PIU) (2000: Annex A6, p. 92)—one of the Prime Minister's support units at 10 Downing Street—summarized what it saw as the problems of the 'traditional' civil service in its report *Wiring it Up*:

- Organizational objectives have a narrow departmental focus, which feeds through to individual objectives and priorities, with clear incentives to keep one's own manager happy, not the manager in another department, leading to collective tunnel vision.
- There is little awareness of the government's strategic priorities, which are not cascaded down effectively.
- Senior civil servants and others do not have incentives to encourage different ways of working, that is to go outside departmental boundaries.

- There are no incentives to join, or contribute to, a project team—the appraisal process does not attach weight to external contributions.
- Performance management and pay focus too much on individual achievement and not enough on team or corporate contribution.

The evidence for such claims is sparse. When one looks for the basis on which these particular statements are made, what is revealed is that the assumptions are drawn from work with 'focus groups', which appear to have featured discussions primarily with senior civil servants about what they thought the problems of the civil service were, sustained by little or no direct empirical evidence.

Further, this perspective is also found in the analysis of the problems of 'public service delivery'. As with the Modernising Government agenda, the problem is seen to lie with the hidebound civil servant, primarily in the middle. Hence a report from the Policy Studies Directorate Centre for Management and Policy Studies (CMPS),[6] formerly a policy unit within the Cabinet Office, entitled 'Better Policy Making' (CMPS 2001: 8) notes: 'The drivers of change are generally at a high-level. This includes Ministers, Permanent Secretaries, and the Senior Civil Service.' In addition, the Office of Public Services Reform (OPSR), another policy unit at 10 Downing Street, commissioned research from a firm of consultants (GHK Consulting) that claimed:

Policy making has sometimes been inward-focused. The objective has been 'to serve Ministers'. This has at times veered towards a focus on policy advice and legislation, rather than on implementation. This is not to suggest that policy has never delivered in the past. Rather, the pressure is now to be seen to deliver public services that make a material difference to people's lives.   (OPSR 2002: 7)

The absence of any specific evidence on which to base such a comment is sharply highlighted by the use of vague descriptions of frequency, sneer quotes, and a double negative in this short passage. It also demonstrates the caricature of civil service organization and behaviour which is often wheeled out to justify the 'modernizing' and managerialist vision of reformers that is rarely, if at all, rooted in the realities of actual operation and practice.

## Patterns of policy bureaucracy

In looking at the civil servants who do the bulk of the policy work in policy bureaucracies we are above all exposing a core paradox in the nature of bureaucracy. Broadly speaking, a bureaucracy is a hierarchical organization; yet the activity of policymaking, which generally requires the mobilization of specialization and expertise, is inherently non-hierarchical.

The paradox derives from Weber's classic theory of bureaucracy.[7] To highlight such a tension in his 'ideal type' of bureaucracy is not to criticize but to use it for what it was originally intended—to detect trends and tensions within systems of government. In Weber's theory hierarchy and expertise are two of the key components of a bureaucratic system. In his oft-quoted ten points defining bureaucracy, hierarchy features strongly. The stipulation that the official operates within a 'firm hierarchy with fixed responsibilities (*Kompetenzen*)' are the second and third characteristics, and being subjected to a 'strong unitary official discipline' is the tenth (Weber 1988: 127). The requirement of 'specialized professional qualification' (*Fachqualifikation*) is characteristic number five and is emphasized consistently throughout his writings on bureaucracy in his major posthumous work *Wirtschaft und Gesellschaft*. The centrality of expertise is summarized in his dictum that 'bureaucratic administration means: rule on the basis of knowledge' (Weber 1988: 129).

Weber (1988: 128-9) explicitly sees hierarchy and expertise as being in conflict. He argues that a non-specialist can 'only control a bureaucratic apparatus to a limited extent'. Although officials may be subordinates, their expertise and knowledge gives them power over their inexpert masters. Since the most inexpert masters in a democratic system are likely to be the elected politicians put in charge of ministries and other parts of the state apparatus, this tension between hierarchy and expertise is at the heart of the dominant question continually posed throughout Weber's analysis (1988: 836) of bureaucracy: how is democracy possible? This issue of the conflict between expertise and dilettantism (Weber 1988: 574ff.) is commonly assumed to be a question that applies to the highest levels of the state apparatus—the interaction between top bureaucrats and politicians. Aberbach et al. (1981: 27) look at this interaction only in the context of officials at the top levels: their 'sampling net was targeted to catch civil servants one to two rungs below the top administrative official in a department' since they have a 'substantial impact on what gets proposed for consideration by governments, what gets passed into law and how laws get implemented' (Aberbach et al. 1981: 24). Yet in many states the conflict between hierarchy and expertise is unlikely to be found at this level since top civil servants are rarely technical experts in any particular policy. Despite their training and belonging to distinctive *corps*, even French civil servants, held by the Fulton Committee to contrast with the 'generalist' civil servant in the UK, are better regarded as generalists who may fit into a range of different jobs (Fulton Committee 1968; Rouban 1999). Senior officials, rather than politicians alone, can be the dilettantes in comparison with their expert subordinates. If a senior official has, say, ten subordinates working under him or her, each with a discrete area of expertise, then, leaving aside the proposition that the ten are grossly underemployed, either the superior has the ability to master the portfolio of detail covered by ten people (this prospect seems unlikely) or the subordinate officials will know things about the issue for which the superior is responsible that the superior does not know.

Moreover this conflict between expertise and hierarchy has implications for democracy not in bureaucracies in general, but in *policy bureaucracies* in particular—organizations responsible for devising and running government programmes as opposed to organizing and delivering them. In the language of administrative science and public administration these administrative units are 'staff' rather than 'line'. Staff units are generally conceptualized as adjuncts somewhere near the top of an organogram. They are a sideways cul-de-sac from a flow of formal authority that, when it involves officials of different ranks, usually flows vertically from top to bottom. While their *conceptualization* is relatively straightforward, their *presentation and identification* are less so. They do not feature in all organizational structures, and are rarely recognized in an organogram. In the UK, policy units are rarely listed separately within the organograms one finds on the websites of Whitehall departments: staff and line units tend to be mixed in the same chart with no distinguishing characteristics. Moreover it is usual in Whitehall for some staff organizations to be constructed on an ad hoc basis. A bill team (Page 2003), for example, is a group of civil servants that exists simply for the life of a piece of legislation; it may (but need not) have a life before and after the legislation and is unlikely to feature in any formal presentation of the work of a government department. We would not claim that staff units should be formally constituted or that every single organization has one. But they are a universal feature of large public organizations with responsibility for developing policy.

What are the effects of this tension? Gouldner (1954: 22) identifies the tension between hierarchy and expertise and places it at the heart of his *Patterns of Industrial Bureaucracy*:

Weber, then, thought of bureaucracy as a Janus-faced organization, looking two ways at once. On the one side, it was administration based on expertise; while on the other it was administration based on discipline. In the first emphasis, obedience is involved as a means to an end; an individual obeys because the rule or order is felt to be the best known method of realising some goal.... In his second conception, Weber held that bureaucracy was a mode of administration in which obedience was an end in itself.

He suggests that different organizations produce different forms of bureaucracy, depending to a significant degree on the importance of expertise. One pattern of bureaucracy in which expertise is less dominant is a 'punishment-centred' bureaucracy in which formal rules and discipline are applied. The second,[8] based on consent and reflecting a higher emphasis on expertise, is a 'representative bureaucracy'.

Yet while the different patterns of bureaucracy—a more hierarchical non-expertise-based punishment-centred bureaucracy and an expertise-based representative bureaucracy in which adherence to formal rules and discipline is less marked—may be produced by the character of the expertise within it,[9] the problem of the conflict between the two is not removed since both patterns can coexist within the same organization. The 'punishment-centred' pattern found among those who worked above the ground in the gypsum mine was different from the representative pattern found among those who worked below the ground, but all were part of the same organization. Despite the importance of the representative model, experts were ultimately subordinate in the whole organization, leading Gouldner (1954: 228) to conclude that 'punishment-centred patterns . . . may have more than an equal share in the conduct of organizational affairs'.

The first central question posed by this conflict in any organization is: how is it possible to direct an expert-based bureaucracy? When asked in the context of a policy bureaucracy, this question is identical to Weber's own question (1988: 836) of how democracy is possible in a bureaucracy. The second question is the corollary of the first: how can expertise be brought to bear within a hierarchical system in which commands can legitimately only come from superiors? Different organizations are likely to have different ways of handling the conflict and thus the answers to the question are likely to differ. It may be that the differences are cultural, and that different organizations within the same country or cultural area tend to have the same or similar answers to this question (cf. Crozier 1964; Hofstede 1979), or perhaps responses are particular to an individual set of organizations or even an individual organization.

These questions of how widespread any particular approach is for adopting particular patterns to cope with the conflict between hierarchy and expertise are ultimately empirical, and we do not have enough empirical material from a big enough range of organizations, in the UK or elsewhere, on which to base much of a conclusion at this stage. By looking at several Whitehall ministries, we are able to throw some light on whether there is a general

Whitehall pattern, but it must be admitted that the numbers we spoke to in individual ministries are small and the questioning did not routinely pursue interministerial differences. Nevertheless, we believe that, if interministerial differences were the mainstay of any answer to our questions, our technique was robust enough at least to give us a strong hint that bureaucratic patterns varied from ministry to ministry.

## Structure of the book

Our central questions are on the one hand to understand the norms and routines by which officials within a policy bureaucracy seek to manage their status as subordinates and still manage to participate effectively and actively in policymaking and, on the other, to understand how, if at all, those in control of them seek to maintain the hold on policymaking that hierarchy and democratic theory expects them to have. We will also be able to offer judgments about how far subordination and democratic control can be maintained. But our central question is not one of assessing degrees of political control, or loss of political control, but understanding the norms and perceptions of those involved.

Chapters 2–6 seek to explore the central theoretical question of democratic control in a policy bureaucracy by presenting a comprehensible, jargon-free, account of how policy bureaucracies work in Whitehall without continual reference to a theoretical framework. Chapter 2 looks at the different types of middle-ranking officials doing policy work: those with middle-level career aspirations who do not expect to be promoted into the Senior Civil Service (SCS); SCS aspirants (those with some hopes to rise into senior positions); and high-flyers (those with great confidence they will progress to an SCS position). It examines the rather haphazard recruitment, educational background, and levels of 'specialization' among such officials. Chapter 3 looks at the range of activities involved in 'policy work'. In particular it looks at three broad types of policy work and illustrates the diverse settings in which they are found—from bilateral bargaining between spending ministries and the Treasury to conducting a major review of the future of the fire services. The three types of policy work are project work (doing a particular policy project such as a White Paper or a piece of legislation); maintenance work (looking after a piece of policy such as a Social Exclusion Unit (SEU) initiative or North Atlantic Treaty Organization (NATO) enlargement); and service work (serving a particular committee such as the Advisory Council on the Misuse of Drugs or running the private office of a minister or permanent secretary).

Chapter 4 examines the argument that the policy work of civil servants outside the SCS is subordinate, merely carrying out the orders of superiors. This chapter shows how the instructions that such officials work to are often imprecise and offer considerable scope for creativity. Moreover the types of issues that officials have to deal with at this level without direct supervision or detailed instruction from above include 'joining up' government, dealing with devolved administrations, human rights, and the European Union (EU). These are not, by any conventional definition, simply matters of unimportant detail. We go on to show that civil servants at this level can also play a significant role in initiating policy. Our argument that officials are not simply concerned with subordinate 'embellishment and detail' of issues settled at a higher level is discussed and illustrated with quotes and examples ranging from wrangling with devolved administrations over the Barnett Formula, handling opponents to genetically modified (GM) crops to rebuilding Stonehenge and introducing 'gay adoptions'. Chapter 5 shows how much policy work is conducted with few direct and specific instructions from on high. Moreover superiors rarely keep a close watch on what middle-ranking officials do, and middle-ranking officials do not pass much through to their superiors for approval. How do officials decide how to carry out their tasks? A variety of mechanisms are used by which a 'ministerial view' is interpreted by officials, including proximate cues (e.g. official reports), ideological extrapolation (identifying strands in government policy and assuming they reflect ministerial preferences), and the important but subtle concept of 'the steer'.

Chapter 6 offers a direct set of answers to the theoretical question of how the conflict within a policy bureaucracy between hierarchy and expertise is managed and the implications for policymaking. In the UK, part of the answer is that the expertise is 'improvised expertise'. Officials are typically in a particular job only a short while, have no training, but they have time and some transferable skills that allow them a mastery of sorts of the issues involved in the policies they handle. Another part of the answer is that hierarchy is exercised 'on demand'—middle-ranking civil servants often have to ask for a 'steer' rather than hierarchy being exercised as a daily part of a senior official's or minister's job. These among other features have implications for the quality of administration and accountability. The chapter explores and compares the UK findings with policy bureaucracies in other countries including France, Germany, Sweden, and the USA.

# Policy Bureaucrats

## Under the hat

In popular parlance, in the UK at least, the term 'civil servant' can evoke three different kinds of image, not all of them particularly flattering, and each somewhat related to class. One image is highlighted by Kingsley (1944): the higher civil service as upper middle class. These people are well paid and inhabit a world of gentlemen (it remains an overwhelmingly male preserve), including gentlemen's agreements, inventiveness with diplomatic language, shared codes of behaviour, and even gentlemen's clubs. This world continues to be evoked by even the most earnest of social science analyses. Bevir and Rhodes (2003), for example, allude to a public school culture of this group when they claim that 'chaps' (a term with upper middle class connotations) remains an important concept in understanding the cultural norms of higher-level Whitehall officials.

A second image is that of a part of the much larger army of public servants who staff the offices of national government services which deal directly with the public or provide 'back office functions'—in the vague phrase of the Gershon Review (Gershon 2004)—including social security, immigration, passports, and tax administration. Often the term 'civil servant' is extended to refer to all public officials who work in offices whether employed by Whitehall, local government, or any other public body. These civil servants are generally less well or even poorly paid, unionized, and prepared to use strike action to seek to assert their rights. This image shares much in common with a traditional view of the British working class, which, with the decline in manufacturing employment, has become increasingly represented in the service sector.

A third image is that of an 'army of faceless individuals in suits and bowler hats—the universal signifier of the English civil servant, understood from here to Beijing'.[10] Their millinery (this aspect of the popular imagery still has them as male although around one-third of middle-ranking civil servants are women) and commuter lifestyle firmly places them among the ranks of the middle class.

The middle can be an awkward position within a bureaucratic system, as Gouldner (1968) has argued. The 'top dogs' have friends because they are powerful, the 'underdogs' have friends because they are powerless, but the middle dogs remain largely friendless. Those at the top make the rules, those at the bottom simply apply them, but what the people in the middle do is harder to understand, as is the mix of creativity and constraint by rules and expectations that characterizes their work. This book explains what they do, but first we must look at who they are. Nobody wears bowler hats any more, and nobody is faceless. If our stereotype of this group is now a complete void, so too is our understanding of what its members are like as a group. This chapter looks at middle-ranking officials from three perspectives. First, it examines who the people in the middle are: what is known of their social background and characteristics. Second, it looks at the rather different types of officials who find themselves in middle grades. Some will end their careers in the middle grades, others are passing through, or expecting to pass through, on the way to higher grades. Third, since we are interested in examining how the expertise of middle-grade officials is harnessed within a hierarchical structure to make policy, we go on to examine what kind of expertise the backgrounds and careers of middle-ranking officials suggest they have.

## Beyond the statistics

We are interested in people doing policy work who are just outside groups generally perceived to be at the top of the civil service. We have reason to believe that at this level below the top is where much of the detail of policy work is done, calling for, as well as engendering, a degree of expertise among those who do it (see Page 2001, 2003). Because so little is known about the group it is necessary to offer some basic description. Such description is hard because the existing statistics—as found in the *Civil Service Statistics* and its predecessors—are patchy. We cannot offer figures about the growth or decline in numbers in this group over time because the bases on which such figures are presented change so frequently that even the shortest of time spans raise insuperable problems of comparability. Moreover, description has got even harder since 1996, after which middle and junior officials have had their grading and pay structures regulated by individual departments rather than the previous practice of being subject to service-wide salary scales. Departments also have some limited discretion about the structure of SCS pay levels (see Baker 2004).

The decentralization of personnel grading means that the classification and nomenclature of the people we are interested in currently varies from department to department. Some departments keep to what is now known as the 'old terms' of Grade 6 as the topmost grade outside the SCS, below which are, in descending order, Grade 7, SEO level and HEO level. In different departments these grades now go under different names. In the Ministry of Defence (MoD), for example, the equivalent to a Grade 7 is a Grade B2 and in the Treasury a Range E. Despite this diversity civil servants generally express their grade in both the contemporary department-specific grade and the common service-wide 'old money' grades of Grade 7, HEO, SEO, and so on. Moreover, for presentational purposes, official civil service statistics still use 'old money' terms, described as 'responsibility levels', to show numbers of staff at different levels of seniority on a service-wide basis (Cabinet Office 2004b). Table 2.1 sets out the 'old money' grades for the SCS as well as the grades below, along with what may be described as the 'antiquated' ranks of the civil service (many of which have survived and are still used) that operated up until the 1980s. Instead of trying to summarize the diverse grading systems in operation in different departments, agencies, and public bodies—the Public and Commercial Services Union (PCS) estimated that there are 170 different systems in 2004[11]— we offer illustrations of the titles of jobs associated with these 'old money' grades.

TABLE 2.1    Grades within the Civil Service

| 'Old money' grades | Antiquated rank | New job titles | Salary (£)* |
|---|---|---|---|
| Grade 1 | Permanent Secretary | Permanent Secretary/Head of Department | 121,100 |
| Grade 2 | Deputy Secretary | Director General | 90,867 |
| Grade 3 | Under-Secretary | Director | 73,762 |
| Grade 4 | Executive Directing Bands | Principal or Senior professional (e.g. Principal Medical Officer) | 62,004 |
| Grade 5 | Assistant Secretary | Director/Deputy Director | 53,541 |
| Grade 6 | Senior Principal | Adviser/Assistant Director/Head of Division | 42,182 |
| Grade 7 | Principal | Adviser/Assistant Director/Head of Branch/Project Manager | 37,321 |
| Senior Executive Officer | Senior Executive Officer | Manager/adviser | 28,883 |

*continues*

TABLE 2.1    *Continued*

| 'Old money' grades | Antiquated rank | New job titles | Salary (£)[*] |
|---|---|---|---|
| Higher Executive Officer | Higher Executive Officer | Manager/officer | 23,511 |
| Higher Executive Officer (Development) | Administration Trainee | "Fast streamers" occupy a range of jobs | 23,822 |
| Executive Officer | Executive Officer/ Higher Clerical Officer | Officer/ Managerial Assistant | 18,638 |
| Administrative Officer | Administrative Officer/Clerical Officer | Administrative Officer | 15,573 |
| Administrative Assistant | Administrative Assistant/Clerical Assistant | Typist/ Receptionist | 13,121 |

*London minimum rates for the different grades as on 1 April 2004. Pay bands for SCS officials (Grade 5 and above) do not coincide neatly with grades. Pay levels for non-SCS officials (Grade 6 and below) are those that apply in the Department for Education and Skills.

*Source*: http://www.dfes.gov.uk/recruitment/pay.cfm and http://www.cabinet-office. gov.uk/civilservice/scs/documents/pdf/HRPGuide.pdf (accessed 11 September 2004).

Table 2.1 also illustrates the minimum salaries associated with each 'old money' grade by presenting those prevailing in the Department for Education and Skills (for grades outside the SCS), the national minima for the four SCS pay bands (which do not always coincide with grade and rank), and for permanent secretaries. For the purposes of this book we are interested in the policy work of those from the 'old money' grades stretching from HEO at the bottom to Grade 6 at the top. Grade 6 is a relatively small group, so in practice the grades we are looking at are the three below that. Despite the extreme diversity in pay-grading systems across departments, all the civil servants interviewed could, when asked, express their current grade in 'old money' and had no trouble identifying themselves as an HEO, SEO, Grade 7, or (rarely) Grade 6.

In 2003 these four grades contained 102,070 officials, made up 23.6 per cent of the total civil service, and as a group were twenty-five times the size of the SCS. The latest available figures giving breakdowns by *individual* grades refer to 1996, but they offer some picture of the distribution within the merged grades presented in Table 2.2. In 1996, 23 per cent of the Grade 6/7 group were in Grade 6 and 77 per cent in Grade 7; 24 per cent of the SEO/HEO group were SEOs—the more senior of the two positions—and 76 per cent were HEOs. In 2003 the HEO group also included 1,164 new entrant fast streamers classed as HEO(D), the bracketed 'D' standing for 'Development' (Hansard 22 July 2004, col. 488W). Fast streamers are generally university graduates who have passed the fast stream entrance exams and Civil Service Selection Board selection and whose careers are in part 'grade-managed' (i.e. they are moved from one post to another and do not apply and compete openly for a new posting) by the departmental human resources office to ensure that capable officials in this category gain the experience needed to progress to the SCS.

What the published statistics tell us about the demographics of this group is limited and largely predictable. It is limited because little data on occupational or socio-economic traits are collected

TABLE 2.2    Grades in the Civil Service (non-industrial) 2003*

| Grade | Number | Percentage |
| --- | --- | --- |
| SCS level | 4,080 | 0.9 |
| Grades 6/7 | 22,050 | 5.1 |
| Senior/Higher Executive Officer | 80,020 | 18.5 |
| Executive Officer | 110,780 | 25.6 |
| Administrative Officer/Assistant | 202,780 | 46.8 |
| Unknown | 13,580 | 3.1 |
| Total | 433,290 | 100.0 |

*Head count.

*Source*: Cabinet Office (2004*b*).

and published. What the statistics tell us is largely predictable because, like middle groups in most hierarchical structures, our middle-ranking civil servants display more characteristics associated with higher socio-economic status groups than those hierarchically below them, and fewer than those above them. Thus they earn more, are more likely to be male, less likely to have a disability, or to come from an ethnic minority than the responsibility levels below, while the relationship is reversed with the status indicators of the SCS.[12]

If we want to know more about middle-ranking officials as a group, we need to go beyond the published statistics and ask them ourselves, and for this research we interviewed 128 of them. However, our sample *cannot be taken as representative of the 102,070 people in these grades*. None of the figures given below can be extrapolated to the wider civil service with any confidence. At best they point to tendencies and relationships between variables. Respondents were included in the sample as they held 'policy' jobs. The precise nature of a 'policy' job is discussed in Chapter 3. However, many officials in middle grades do not do 'policy' jobs. HEOs also do 'operational' jobs, that is, acting as a health and safety inspector or running local job centres. While a Grade 7 is generally a managerial post, it is not necessarily a 'policy' post. For example, the Superintendent of the Royal Parks Constabulary is a Grade 7 civil servant (Appendix A discusses the sample of civil servants in more detail). Hence the grading system does not allow one to determine how many such officials are 'policy' officials, even if it were possible to come up with an accepted definition of 'policy'. These problems aside, what do our interviews tell us about this group?

## Careers in the middle

### Pathways into the service

Being an HEO or a Grade 7 in the civil service is not like being an astronaut or a train driver—people in these positions are unlikely to be there as a result of a long-standing ambition. The most common way of joining the civil service was by graduate entry—either through a successful application to the fast stream or through another form of competition—usually at the EO level. For those who entered the civil service shortly after a bachelor's or higher degree through the fast stream, the attractions of a policy career were likely to be emphasized as a reason for joining the civil service.

I have a biochemistry degree (Manchester) and Ph.D. (Cambridge). I had thought about the civil service after my first degree. After I did my Ph.D. I decided I did not want to go into academia and I was attracted to government work—the policy aspect appealed to me, especially working for ministers, so I applied to the fast stream. In January 2000, I came into the fast stream and into the Department of Trade and Industry (DTI).

However, for the rest, including those expecting SCS promotion who had not entered straight after university, there was a great diversity of reasons for joining the service. One of the most common was to avoid what were perceived to be either boring jobs or those with no prospects. As one put it: 'I graduated from Liverpool in Business Studies. I went into hotel management, but I got bored with watching people eat.' Another said:

I graduated [without honours] in 1983 ... [and] ... was attracted to the civil service. I applied to be a junior manager in an EO grade. I did not get through. I then went on to do lots of different things, though I did not have a proper job. I saw an advertisement.... I think this just said 'civil servant at clerical officer grade'. I don't remember being asked which department I wanted to go in. I got a letter saying that I had been allocated to [this one].

Similarly a lawyer who made the switch to the civil service, now in a Grade 7 policy job, commented: 'I was in practice as a solicitor for fifteen years and got fed up with clients.'

Coincidence and happenstance were very common explanations for how respondents ended up in the civil service. An HEO in his thirties describes his pathway:

How did I come to the job? After I ... studied sociology and public administration ... I worked with [a] cancer charity—a terrific charity. There was a chap from the Department of Health [DoH] there on secondment. I was only doing temping stuff. When I finished there the chap got in touch with me. He said: 'I know you are unemployed, will you temp for us?' I had a couple of months' work, I thought. I had casual status. I carried on and got contracts for a year and eighteen months. It got to the point where people realized I could do more than the filing. Even with my casual status I was given more responsibility. It got to the stage where I was working for a woman in a unit where it was just the two of us. She wanted to make it permanent, so it had to go to a special board to allow me to be appointed without the job being advertised. I was very drifty after my degree. I came into this more by luck than judgement. I could quite easily have left. I did not want to do filing for the DoH. But I caught up quite quickly with people of my age who had studied and gone into the civil service.

Perhaps the most unusual pathway was described by another HEO in his thirties:

I fell into the civil service quite by accident. I was not one of your normal career paths [joining shortly after graduating from a degree course]. I did GCSEs and went on to do A levels, but I did not do too well at them. I had discovered the joys of women and drink. I went on doing lots of jobs—about thirty-five jobs in seven years. Then I decided to go to university at the age of twenty-five. I did history and politics at [a new university]. During that time my stepbrother got a job at Buckingham Palace (just after a bit of Windsor Castle burned down). He got me a job at the Buckingham Palace summer opening. I was promoted and ended up in charge of about fifty people looking after security and being nice to visitors. A by-product of this was that I got security clearance to work in the civil service. When I left I went to work for a temporary agency which specialized in civil service placement and worked for the DTI for about two years. But they would not let me in as a permanent civil servant because the computer they used to sift applications said I was 'not suitable'. I applied to other departments, one of them was the old Department of the Environment, Transport and the Regions (DETR). They accepted me as an EO. I was promoted two years later to HEO, so hopefully I will go on from there to SEO or Grade 7—I'm looking for those sort of jobs now.

Other unusual routes into the civil service included a Grade 7 who had previously been in a professional occupation but whose failing eyesight prevented him from continuing, although his skills could be used in the public sector; and a person working in a newspaper shop near a commuter railway station who got to know one customer who advised her to apply to the government department he was working in that happened to be recruiting at the time.

## Terminus or stepping stone?

With career paths pursued once they are in the civil service, we can divide the people we interviewed into two broad groups. First, are those for whom a senior position in the middle ranks, i.e. *outside* the SCS, is broadly accepted as the highest grade likely to be achieved before leaving the civil service, whether through retirement or resignation. We may call this group 'officials with middle-ranking career aspirations'. They made up just over one-third (34 per cent) of the officials we interviewed.[13] Second, are those who entertain serious expectations that they might be promoted to an SCS position and continue their careers there. This group can be divided into two: those who have a high expectation, in some cases bordering on certainty, that they will progress to an SCS post, whom we may call 'high-flyers' (39 per cent of the people we interviewed); and those with less certainty, whom we may call 'SCS promotion aspirants' (26 per cent). These groups are not hard and fast. Our interviews offer at best snapshots of respondents' states of mind on this issue: people who have high expectations may have them dashed over time, and those without such expectations may develop them (and we came across instances of both). Departmental human resources offices, as we will see below, have schemes to bring on talented and experienced personnel. However, for the purposes of understanding the occupational group we are talking about, it is useful to divide them into these three groups.[14]

Officials with middle-ranking career aspirations include those who are happy to remain within the middle grades. One Grade 7 in his early forties, working in an office well beyond commuting distance from London, argued that part of the bargain of working where he worked was the quality of life. He pointed out of the window to a residential area close by and said: 'That's where I live. It takes me a few minutes to walk to work.' He added, 'You don't get to stay in [this town] and move to SCS. You take the Alan Milburn option', referring to the Labour Health Secretary who had resigned in June 2003, the day before the interview, giving the reason that he could better enjoy the benefits of bringing up a young family. An SEO in his late twenties argued:

I cannot stay in this job—that way is burnout mode. The stress levels are unhealthy. Most Grade 7s around here have been off long-term sick at some stage. For health reasons I won't do it. I want to work outside in another job. I have been asked to apply for a Grade 7 twice. I would not apply in [this field of work]. It is too stressful. I have two young kids and I like to see them.

Another Grade 7 in his early forties was frank that he did not want more responsibility:

I'm not really a career person. I enjoy what I do and when I have stopped enjoying it I move on and find somewhere to go that I enjoy.... In the past I must say that I felt a bit overstretched in my previous post, this one I feel I can juggle the balls without getting overstressed. In a higher grade I knew there were more pressures on you, but they affected me more than I thought they would. At [my age] I am not going to have much option to move elsewhere. I could go to a Non-Departmental Public Body (NDPB) but I don't have it in mind to go for a career change. By default I'll probably see out my career [in this department], I could move to a parallel post. I have no particular objective in mind by way of targets for my career.

Yet it is not accurate to suggest that officials with middle-ranking career aspirations have limited ambitions. Several HEOs and SEOs spoke with enthusiasm of their plans for advancement within middle grades. As an HEO in her thirties put it:

I like this job, though I did not like the [job I came from] where I was treated like I was just a secretary. [My Grade 7 is] very good on that—very supportive and good to learn from. I'm starting to look for a position. The last promotion board was in 1996, after that it was Job-Specific Selection. I'll stay on here until I'm able to look at an SEO grade.

The category of officials with middle-ranking career aspirations also includes others less resigned to the opportunities available. An SEO union representative in his forties argued:

There is a pretty big division between the senior civil servants and the rest. Grade 7s feel especially blocked. They feel you have to have a high-flying background or be recruited from the outside to break into it. Even if you are very good at your job at Grade 7 the chances of getting into it are small. So they think, 'What is the point?'

A few officials endorsed such a view, including many of those who could be classified as SCS aspirants, uncertain about their prospects of promotion to an SCS post, but having some expectation that this is possible.

High-flyers are more confident. Some of them are career-managed—groomed for posts within SCS. Although they are likely to reach the SCS this can never be taken for granted. Those who enter the fast stream are almost universally upbeat about their chances, and while many were not thinking about their future in the SCS, but rather building up their 'portfolio' (the range of jobs that would make up an attractive curriculum vitae for promotion purposes), some were confident. A fast streamer in her late twenties, at HEO level, noted:

I would hope to reach the SCS in a short period. I decided I did not want to go in the European fast stream and decided I would rather influence Whitehall from a European aspect rather than be part of the European institutions.

Thus SCS promotion is not only a clear prospect for many fast streamers but also a priority objective. Indeed as one respondent suggested: 'I would not have come into the civil service if I had not got into the fast stream, I would have looked at other careers.'

Yet it is not only civil service fast streamers who face their prospects for promotion with confidence. There are varieties of grade management schemes within different departments. The MoD has a Means of Identifying and Developing Individual Talent (MIDIT) scheme, which seeks to nurture civil servants working in the department. One of them, at SEO level, saw his career developing thus:

In MIDIT you move every two years. [My Grade 7] has already told me he'll put a 'fitted for promotion' on my report. On the basis of one 'fitted' you can go to the assessment centre. Generally they don't accept people with fewer than two, but can accept you with one. I could end up doing another term as [an SEO] before I'd realistically be looking at a Grade 7.

There are similar schemes in other departments, such as the Accelerated Development Programme in the DTI and the Intensive Development Programme in the Home Office.

In addition, even those outside any career management scheme can realistically aspire for a similar career to a fast streamer. A Grade 7 in his thirties, a graduate, described his career thus:

I applied to the civil service through the EO entrance scheme. I went to [an NDPB where I worked for its head]. After five years there, and at the [suggestion of the NDPB's head]—he wanted to help my career—I went on a secondment to ... the Home Office. I liked it [and eventually negotiated a clean transfer] ... I like to move from job to job but ... I feel I need to develop a specialism. I'm ambitious. This might take me to the areas which could take me further. But I don't think this job will be my specialism. I cannot say how long it will take to get to the SCS. Some people have been in Grade 7 for 15–20 years. For me that is unacceptable—I would not want that for myself. I expect it in around four years—it could be a bit longer.

Indeed, several officials who joined the civil service as EOs straight from university saw themselves as little different from those who joined through the fast stream. Two who had been turned down for the fast stream entry applied through this route and then applied to join the fast stream as internal candidates. A Grade 7 around the age of thirty, who had joined as an EO straight from university, and who was 'proud' that he had made it to Grade 7 in six years, argued that direct EO entry was likely to become more popular: 'There are more people coming in as EOs as there are more people coming into universities—that is an interesting product of the expansion of universities.'

The *SCS promotion aspirants* have less confidence about their chances of rising to an SCS position, but still entertain the possibility. A Grade 7 in her thirties is fairly typical of this group:

I'm a bit of a fatalist—if it happens, it happens. A friend of mine was temporarily promoted when someone left from a Grade 7 to an SCS post and then later it was confirmed. I see it as being in the right place at the right time.

Another Grade 7 around the same age was unsure of her prospects:

[*Interviewer: Is it easy to get into SCS?*] Not terribly. I have been on a pilot [fast stream–type] scheme. There were fifty women on this year-long programme designed to bring on talent—recruiting from people who could get into SCS. The government has targets for women in the SCS. But even so, I would still say it is quite difficult. I think it will be some time before I am willing to attempt it. I came through the ranks quite quickly to Grade 7. I'm not sure whether being a woman helped via positive discrimination, or hindered this.

*Que sera sera* also sums up the views of an HEO in her thirties who had been through an internal fast track scheme:

I should say that in [this department] they have recently set up [a departmental] fast track scheme. You go on it for three years and have a post a year. You go through a selection and interviewing process. Then they look at your previous jobs, where the gaps are in your career and they put you in a position accordingly. [*Interviewer: Do you expect to be thinking about an SCS position?*] At the end of three years you are expected to make it to Grade 7 and then you see how things go.

Moreover, such views are often tinged with doubts, especially among those not in the fast stream. The importance of grade management can be seen in the words of an official who is not on such a scheme:

[In this department] we are supposed to be a mixed economy of applications and grade management. But unless I can persuade someone to grade-manage me into a position I could still be here for years to come. It sounds like a chip on my shoulder but they go for the younger people to grade-manage.

When asked about her chances for promotion, a Grade 7 said: 'If you are not a fast streamer—they are rather different types and I would have been on a different rung if I had been... [*tails off*].' The advantages of being a fast streamer, she added, can be long-lasting since once they have reached Grade 7 ex-fast streamers are still largely looked on more favourably 'in many circles regardless of ability at the grade merely by virtue of having been a fast streamer compared with non–fast streamers, in the way that men may have been said once to have had (no longer, I hope) [an advantage] over women'.

Different types of careers bring people into the middle grades. Our threefold distinction points to different expectations of the job, but only from the perspective of whether it is a stepping stone to an SCS post or whether a career can be expected to end within this set of grade bands. While it is currently fashionable in political science to portray incentive structures and motivations as explanations of behaviour, it remains to be seen whether we may hold any particularly firm expectations about the impact of such career aspirations on actual behaviour among our officials. It was not the central ambition of this research to look at such possible effects of incentive structures, and no clear quantitative evidence for them can be given here. We can offer only our impressions. Questions about career histories and ambitions were generally asked at the end of the interviews, and it was impossible to guess from the degree of enthusiasm or commitment expressed in connection with the work that the respondent did (usually the first and largest part of the interview) what they said about their chances for promotion. Thus, an Oxbridge graduate who had entered by the fast stream and reached Grade 7 with every chance of reaching the SCS half-joked: 'I have been in [this] grade eight years in January. [This department] likes to keep its Grade 7s in that grade until they are all bitter and twisted.' While a Grade 7, who spoke in the most enthusiastic terms about her job, and how she had worked extra hours to develop and deliver a useful innovation that she herself had identified, was a non-graduate who had been in the civil service for twenty-three years, and her chances of promotion to the SCS on the face of it seemed more remote than those of the Oxbridge graduate. If there is any systematic impact of career incentives on forms of behaviour or even approach to the job, they were not detected by our interviews.

## Education and expertise

In what way might officials at this level be considered to have expertise? The classic way of defining expertise in studies of bureaucracy is through looking at educational backgrounds and qualifications. Just as the Oxbridge classics degree has traditionally marked top UK officials as generalists and the dedicated *Ecole Nationale d'Administration* (ENA) training has created the impression that their French counterparts are specialists (see Suleiman 1978 for an alternative view), does the educational background of our middle-ranking officials suggest they might be more specialized than their superiors?

A university degree is not a prerequisite for a policy job in the middle grades of the civil service. As an undated fact sheet from the Department for Transport (*c.* 2003) states:

Higher executive officers (HEOs) should have either a 2:2 degree (or equivalent), or a minimum of three years' policy development, and staff, resource or project management experience. . . . Team leaders [Grade 7s] must have either a 2:2 degree (or equivalent), or a minimum of five years' policy development, and staff, resource or project management experience.[15]

Grade 7s without degrees did not consider themselves to be particularly unusual. In fact the only person without a degree who commented that not having a degree marked him off from colleagues was an HEO in the MoD who explained: 'I am a bit unusual as it is only normally graduates who are desk officers.'

However, 76 per cent of our respondents had a degree and, as one would expect, this differed between different types: 98 per cent of the high-flyers, 69 per cent of the SCS aspirants, and 56 per cent of the officials with middle-ranking career aspirations had degrees. Perhaps the most striking feature of our interviews as far as educational background is concerned (see Table 2.3) is the relatively low proportion of officials who had university degrees when they joined the service and the numbers who left university before completion of their degree course. However, these features are only striking if we expect officials at this grade to resemble the higher civil service in its overwhelmingly graduate composition. Compared with the population at large, officials in middle grades are highly educated. Only 16.3 per cent of the working-age population in the UK in 2003 had a degree; in London, where the majority of interviews was conducted, this figure was 24.7 per cent (see Office for National Statistics 2004). Moreover the number of officials who dropped out of university—6 per cent of those interviewed—is unremarkable, as the dropout rate for higher education institutions in the UK has remained around 17 per cent since the early 1990s (Hansard 3 March 2004: col 995W).

While the proportion of Grade 7s with no university degree (8/56 or 14 per cent) was lower than that of HEOs and SEOs (17/38 or 45 per cent), it is still possible to reach Grade 7 without a university degree. One official from the Department for Culture Media and Sport (DCMS) explained that managing to reach Grade 7 was a generational matter:

I am a non-graduate. I have been in the civil service a long time. I am one of the generation that came in just before everyone went to university. The idea was that women should be educated but not have careers. The difference today is interesting. You talk to women graduates in the department and they have real difficulty in understanding how hard it was. It was only in the 1970s that the system stopped whereby women had to face the decision of whether to marry or stay in the Foreign Office.

The HEO from the MoD quoted above (p. 32) had been promoted relatively quickly despite not having a degree:

[*Interviewer: Does not being a graduate make life difficult for you?*] Not really. The way the policy area works is that we have a number of fast

TABLE 2.3   Educational background of officials interviewed

| Qualification | Number | Percentage |
| --- | --- | --- |
| Higher degree | 14 | 13 |
| Bachelor degree before joining civil service | 78 | 70 |
| Bachelor degree from Oxbridge before joining civil service | 21 | 19 |
| Did university degree while a civil servant | 7 | 6 |
| Dropped out of university | 7 | 6 |
| No university degree | 27 | 24 |
| Total valid responses | 112 | 138* |

*Column adds up to over 100% as multiple codings are possible.

*Source*: Compiled from interviews (see Appendix).

streamers . . . in a series of one-year postings. They tend to join at 22–23 and run up to Grade 7. They join at C2 [HEO level]. For my sins I was promoted to C2 at 22. I was in a reasonably good position. I have experience and I am not suffering and am unlikely to suffer as a consequence. At least I don't think so. The pyramid does narrow when you get closer to the top.

While the figures suggest that those with a degree are more likely to reach Grade 7, a degree does not appear to be decisive in achieving seniority in a middle-ranking career.

When we looked at promotion from Grade 7 to the SCS without a degree, views were mixed about how much further a career could progress. A Treasury official in this position was already looking for a higher level job: 'I went straight into the civil service from school. I did not go to university—I had an opportunity to once. . . . I'll be looking for promotion in two to three years time, a Grade 5 I hope.' Whereas an official from the Office of the Deputy Prime Minister (ODPM) said:

If the right job came up I'd probably do it. But I am now feeling that the lack of a degree would be a barrier to my further promotion. That is a reality. I recognize I also have a lot of outside interests—I'm not one for late nights in the office.

Empirically, the more sceptical response is better founded: 80 per cent of Grade 5s in the civil service have university degrees.[16]

It is possible to acquire a degree after joining the civil service—seven of our respondents did so. Different departments at different times offered different types of support for their officials who wanted to study for a degree:

I applied and got a place at the London School of Economics. . . . The MoD gave me three years' unpaid leave—they did not sponsor me as what I was proposing was not directly in their interest. I half-thought that when I graduated I would do something different. When I graduated I had built up loads of debts and thought 'well, there's a . . . job waiting for me' so I came back to the Department in 1991.

Another official, without a bachelor's degree, was supported by the Department for Work and Pensions (DWP):

In the meantime I did an MBA [Masters in Business Administration] sponsored by the Department. In fact it was a CIPFA [Chartered Institute of Public Finance and Accountancy] postgraduate Diploma in Business and Finance. I got accepted on this as I was an HEO and the university concerned said 'that's degree status'. It was done by distance learning. Since my tutor insisted on setting the assignments to MBA standards, I had enough credits to be accepted on the MBA course for the final year.

There appeared to be no general pattern to the support offered to pursue university study; rather those who had asked about it believed it to be something decided on a case-by-case basis.

## Qualifications and expertise

While the majority of middle-ranking officials have a university education, it is not a degree that makes them specialists. Middle-ranking officials are *not subject specialists*. A fairly common ice-breaking comment at the very start of an interview was that we were public administration scholars and not specialists in hospital finance, animal diseases, or whatever subject covered the respondent's current job. The respondent's reply was invariably 'neither am I'. A fast streamer was asked whether he had any expertise in the rather technical area for which he was responsible. 'Absolutely not' came the reply, 'I have a classics degree from Cambridge and an M.Phil. in Economic and Social History from Oxford. I have never had any expertise on anything I have worked on.'

Even those with degrees that appear close to their current jobs, making them prime candidates for the label 'specialists', pointed out that appearances can be deceptive. As one Grade 7 with a degree in economics put it:

I started off at the Department of the Environment (DoE) in a department [and a post] where I have [a degree] which seems to have a relevance for my job. [*Interviewer: Does your degree actually help you in your job?*] No! Certainly not in terms of specifics. Yes, I might be able to read a table more easily—there are things that are useful. [*Interviewer: But not in the sense that you say 'I remember the lecture on this or reading about this'?*] That's right.

This view was echoed by the official who pointed out: 'Economics is useful for my job. It is useful when you come to ask the economists, on whom we rely to get costings.' But she added: 'The sort of economics you learn in university has very little to do with the sort of practical economics we are dealing with here.' And another with an economics degree suggested: 'In this job it is not strictly economist tools I apply, but the tools and skills you have acquired as an economist come in useful.'

 The apparent perversity of personnel offices in tending to appoint people with educational qualifications to posts for which they appeared less qualified came up in several interviews:

I have been with [this department] for getting on for twenty years. Yes, I came straight after university. Joined as an EO. I have a degree in . . . economics from Exeter and it was useful up to a point. I don't get involved with economic things though—the economists do that. I joined the same day as a woman with a degree in statistics. They sent her to economics and me to statistics. I think personnel might not do that now.

A linguist we interviewed had just found a job better suited to her talents:

I wanted to get back on track into European issues. I speak six languages and don't use any in my current job, so looking for something in which I could use my skills was important, otherwise it is a waste.

Another who was frequently representing her department in the EU said:

I did French and German ... and I trained as a translator. ... [T]he only time I usually speak French in Brussels is when I order in a restaurant. Some documents ... are first published in French. And I have written a summary of [a] paper I wrote in French. I have a French tutor who said that I should be good enough to write it, and I did it, and it was OK, just needed a couple of tweaks.

Another linguist pointed to a double coincidence in being appointed to her current job, which involved compiling statistics from different parts of the UK, including devolved administrations, for an international body:

I speak French, my husband is French. I have a degree in English language and literature from Glasgow University, but nothing technical. [*Interviewer: Was it coincidence that you have French and end up responsible for this job?*] Yes, happenstance. It is happenstance too that I am Scottish and get to work with the Scottish Executive. Scotland is treated as part of the UK for the purpose of statistics, although Scotland has a separate seat [on the international body]; Wales and Northern Ireland are happy for me to take responsibility. So I deal with people in the NI executive, the Welsh Executive, the Scottish Executive.

Many of those who had joined one of the specialized 'fast track' schemes, whether European, or scientific, or who had joined as specialists such as economists, tended to find the need to become more generalist. A scientific fast streamer commented:

In some posts you need to be a scientist, but clearly not this one. It could be done by a generalist. I hope to get involved in science policy. I want to stay in [this department] but move to a different part.

An economics fast streamer said:

I joined as an economist. There are two ways you can go. You can go on as an economist and stay put. But there is a limit even in a department the size of MAFF [Ministry of Agriculture, Forestry and Fisheries] or DEFRA [Department for Environment, Food and Rural Affairs] on how many times you can go round the economics department [meaning getting different jobs specifically for economists in the department] and then you look for something different. I felt like getting out.

There was only one exception among our respondents to this general principle that educational qualifications had little bearing on subsequent careers:

My [science] degree is very relevant. I joined . . . on the [technical] inspectorate side, not the policy side. I worked as an inspector for seven years, then got an HQ job, then got promoted to a Grade 7 equivalent. Then four years ago I went on the SPATS (Senior Professionals Administrative Training Scheme) at Sunningdale. The idea is to induct technical and scientific people into policy work, either for a management role in the science and technology area or to allow you to move into policy. Part of that involved a secondment to a policy role, and I applied for the job and got it.

But he realized it was unusual that he had a degree directly related to his current work:

Yes it is unusual for the UK civil service, but I am similar to all the other people [from other countries] on the [EU] standing committee [on which I sit]—they have a technical background. I am different from my predecessors in this job who have had history degrees and such like.

If middle-ranking officials are experts, it is not because of their education. One official described his job, dealing with policy related to food, as requiring technical expertise:

This is a technical post—the level of knowledge about the issue has been all-encompassing to survive and converse with stakeholders.

Yet he was not a graduate. So while the clear majority has one, a university degree rarely serves as the basis for a specialized career covering a particular subject, even for fast streamers whose early careers are managed to allow them to learn specific sets of skills by placing them in appropriate positions. Moreover many degrees, often believed to be technical or 'specialized' such as economics, have little direct bearing on the tasks that policy officials carry out in their everyday work beyond offering more diffuse skills such as reasoning or reading a statistical table. On what other bases might the expertise of our officials rest?

## Specialization and mobility

The expertise of our middle-ranking officials might result from their on-the-job experience. Whatever one has studied, it is unlikely to provide the technical grounding for everyday policy work in the civil service. University study rarely involves direct experience of the issues and questions that policy work brings with it: there are few degree courses that specialize in handling a bill in the House of Commons or deciding what to place at the top of a minister's pile of papers. However, it is possible to gain expertise through practical specialization—staying in the same job or moving between jobs that cover similar types of issues.

### Interdepartmental mobility

One outward sign of this kind of specialization is the general norm that officials interviewed made their careers, at least up to the middle grades they occupied, within the same department. Determining whether an official was in the 'same department' requires some interpretation. There have been several reorganizations of government departments so it is possible for an official in, say, the DWP to have worked in health policy—now covered by a separate department—without having applied for any form of transfer since both types of work were contained in the old Department of Health and Social Security, which was created in 1968 and split in 1988. We will see how staying in the same ministry does not necessarily mean specialization, but let us first examine the evidence of interministerial mobility.

Of the 114 officials on whom we have data, 40 (35 per cent) changed ministry or organization at least once in their careers. Some of these instances of mobility are unspectacular. Two DWP officials worked on social security issues for the Parliamentary

Commissioner for Administration (PCA) and a third for the Benefits Agency. Yet others are more substantial, and include periods on loan in other departments. While there are too few in each ministry for us to say with any confidence that there is any departmental pattern, twenty of the forty mobile civil servants were found in just three departments: the Treasury, the ODPM, and the DTI.[17] These departments, moreover, had officials who had really switched between different parts of Whitehall.

However, the length of time in the same department is not much of an indicator of subject specialization. It is possible to have diverse jobs within the same department: handling immigration in the Home Office is commonly combined in a career with other issues such as drugs or money laundering. Moreover, it is possible to do a similar job and still move departments: for example, the official in a spending ministry dealing with finance issues who moved to the Treasury to deal with his successor in the spending ministry.

## Job mobility

One of our respondents remarked that it is more usual for a Continental European official to be a subject specialist, and a specialist who stays in the job for a long time. This point was also mentioned by several officials who worked alongside others from EU member states. As one put it:

The big difference is that different countries send different types of people. The Greeks send very senior people—they cannot, it seems, authorize more junior people to come. Some countries send their real technical experts. . . . Some people have been in their jobs for ages. One of the first meetings I went to everyone was in tears as one of the people who had been there twenty-five years was leaving! Can you imagine that, twenty-five years? Mind you the fact that our people are always changing is something the Commission always complains about.

We occasionally came across a high degree of subject specialization in the UK. One respondent who had moved between departments argued: 'I have broad knowledge of social security as I have spent my entire career in social security and have experience in all sorts of specific benefits.' How common is it to find such subject specialization and expertise in the UK? The social security specialist just quoted went on to say that the job she was in at the moment covered a social security issue 'I don't have that much experience in.... I [have to] rely on my team. We can pool our experience. I very much rely on them for expertise'. We can offer a better assessment of the subject expertise of our officials if we look more closely at their levels of experience in their current jobs.

One way of assessing experience is the length of time officials stay in the same job. While they might not be subject specialists when they come to the post, they may develop an expertise in the topic for which they are responsible once they have been in the job for a year or two. Yet most officials had been in their positions for a relatively short time when they were interviewed—on average seventeen months. While the sample of respondents is not random, the figure of seventeen months suggests that, in the absence of substantial bias in favour of interviewing people in earlier or later stages of their incumbency of a particular post, around just under three years is an average stint in any particular job. The figure of three years fits the popular conception among many officials of how long one should stay in a job in order to build up subject expertise and show an ability to 'stick at one thing'. An SEO in the Department for Education and Skills (DfES) replied:

How long will I stay in the job? Usually you don't stay for more than three years. But I do enjoy this job, and I get a lot of variety in it. You get to meet people outwith the department and you get out quite a bit, so I am quite happy in this position.

While three years was the most common reply when such a generalization was offered, others saw their careers developing in shorter episodes. A Grade 7 in the Home Office finished a lengthy description of his career, which divided neatly into several two-year chunks as follows:

[Then] I was in the Sentencing and Offences Unit. I was an HEO there. This was purely a policy job. I was two years in there and then went to the Juvenile Offenders Unit. I was two years there . . . and moved from there to Modernization and Strategy for two years. I'm a two-year person.

And another wanted to stay longer in each post:

I joined the civil service as an EO. In terms of career progression going this route means that I lost out by a couple of years [over people joining the fast stream]. I did an HEO job, but did it for four years. I think it suited me more. Fast streamers have a heavy turnover of jobs and my preference is to stick at things for longer and get into nitty-gritty detail. I did not plan it this way, but on reflection this suits me better than zapping something for a year and moving on. Not wanting to rush about and wanting to develop relationships with the outside world are disadvantages.

The estimate of how long one is expected to stay in a job is likely to reflect in part whether one's career is being grade-managed or not: high-flyers consistently pointed out 'you are expected to stay for 12–18 months'. One high-flyer expressed the opinion, common among them, that moving a lot was the sign of a career in the ascendancy:

You are supposed to move a lot. I am one of the youngest of the fast streamers. How quickly you get promoted depends upon your competence and experience. The norm is to have three or four postings before promotion. Some get promoted in their second year. These tend to be the ambitious ones.

Tables 2.4 and 2.5 show that high-flyers in general and HEO(D)s in particular are likely to have shorter periods in the same jobs. High-flyers were likely to have been in post for fourteen months on average at the time of interview as opposed to nineteen months for officials with middle-ranking career aspirations, and HEO(D)s in particular were in post for eleven months.

HEO(D)s who spent more than eighteen months in one post tended to be in jobs regarded as particularly attractive, including the private office of a minister, or better secretary of state (among other things managing the flow of information going to the minister from the department), or on a team developing policy for

TABLE 2.4    Average period in post at the time of interview (months)

| By grade | |
|---|---|
| Grade 7 | 18 |
| SEO | 18 |
| HEO | 16 |
| HEO(D) | 11 |
| By type | |
| High-flyer | 14 |
| SCS aspirant | 19 |
| Middle-ranking aspirant | 19 |
| Average (all groups) | 17 |

*Source*: Compiled from interviews (see Appendix).

TABLE 2.5    Length of time in current post

| Length of time | Number | Percentage |
|---|---|---|
| Over 36 months | 4 | 4 |
| 25–36 months | 13 | 14 |
| 13–24 months | 29 | 32 |
| 9–12 months | 21 | 23 |
| Under 9 months | 23 | 26 |
| Total | 90 | 100 |

*Source*: Compiled from interviews (see Appendix).

major legislation (a bill team—see Page 2003). Such jobs are supposed to be good postings for a fast streamer since they provide exposure to senior officials and politicians, show the ability to work on one's own initiative, demonstrate that one can operate at a high level within the department, and also provide insight into how different parts of the department work. As one fast streamer put it:

Bill teams are a good way of getting promotion if you do it well because everyone notices. There is lots of contact with ministers, contact across the department and with other departments and generally quite prestigious and can be quite fun in a pressurized sort of way.

Another fast streamer, at the time a Grade 7, said: 'But I cannot see how you can function as a senior civil servant without having done it. You get to see the pressures operating on ministers and senior civil servants.' One official in a secretary of state's private office told us:

It is a long time since someone was not promoted out of private office. Sometimes you see people promoted out of it and you wonder why [since they don't appear to be that talented]. It is not the best place to develop the sorts of skills that get mentioned—drafting, doing legislation, delivery—but in terms of understanding what happens at that level and where ministers are coming from it is absolutely invaluable, vital.

Another fast streamer plotted the contribution of working in a private office to his career in confident terms:

I did three jobs as a fast streamer for less than one year each. I was just over a year in private office as an HEO(D) and eighteen months as a Grade 7. I'd need to do another two Grade 7 jobs if I pushed it [to get promotion to SCS]. There are a few more boxes I need to tick.

The general rule is one should not spend too long in any job, but in some kinds of high-status jobs, staying on a little longer is not likely to be harmful to a career and can indicate desirable qualities in an official aspiring for promotion. A major piece of legislation may take over two years from inception to Royal Assent and remaining with it throughout can indicate staying power and competence a secretary of state who wants to hang on to a high-flyer in private office for more than the usual eighteen months is giving a signal that the official concerned is good at dealing with issues at the highest level within a department.

However, while there is some variation in how long being in the same job is perceived to be good for one's career, it is variation of a short period. The evidence suggests that to be in the same job for more than three years starts to look bad for anyone who wants any career advancement, and to be in a job for much more than two years would be worrying for someone hoping for rapid career advancement unless the job has other obvious career advantages.

## Experience

Staying in the job for a long time is not necessarily the same as specializing in a particular topic. Jobs change even if their incumbents remain the same. The official who had been in the same post the longest—five years—was doing something different at the time of interview from what he was doing five years before.

I have sat in the same seat for the past five years and the job has formed around me. Three years ago the post was set up and I was counting the qualifications of nurses before they were recruited.

His current position dealt with wider national and international recruitment of National Health Service (NHS) staff. Another, whose post gave her responsibility for the development of Stonehenge, came to the post when it was something completely different:

I started this job on loan—I responded to an advertisement, and at that point the branch was about world heritage—dealing with the UN and the Council of Europe. The other side of the work involved casework issues. It was in some archaic legislation which gave people the right of appeal to the Secretary of State. And I had Stonehenge. It was a bit like a cuckoo—it took over the world, or my world anyway.

While one might not stay in the same post for long, it is still possible to develop expertise in a particular topic by doing several different jobs related to it. For example, one Grade 7 described his specialism, albeit through pointing out he had moved away from it, using nautical terms:

I took th[is] job [in local government modernization] because it was originally dealing with promoting community leadership and sustainability and these areas are my career anchor. The job changed after I got here—I joined two years ago. I am now returning to DEFRA to work on [a farming issue].

The term 'career anchor' refers to a core personal subject specialization, which officials can nurture and maintain even though they may not always work within their specialism. The career anchor has in the past few years entered the terminology, in a minor way, of human resource management in the civil service as offering a compromise between subject specialization and generalization.[18] What evidence is there of officials having career anchors?

One way of assessing the degree to which this idea of officials being 'anchored' held true is to see how many officials had direct experience of the area in which they work. Fewer than one-third of respondents (31 per cent) had previous experience doing similar work in the same area (Table 2.6). This figure of 31 per cent possibly overstates the degree to which policy expertise is the basis for recruiting an official to a particular post (or possibly for an official applying for a particular post) since 'previous experience' refers only to a related *topic*, although the *type of job* might be different. An HEO describes how she came to her job working on pensions:

I had worked on private pensions for five years, then I moved to the international side of the department, general EU, but because I knew about pensions, everything to do with pensions came to my desk. I came back upstairs [to pensions] although I was working on a different area of pensions. Before that I was dealing with equal treatment—that was a main European angle on pensions. The pensions section up here would normally have done that, but as I was downstairs I got it—your specialisms

TABLE 2.6    Officials' previous experience of similar work

|  | No. of Respondents | No. with experience of similar work | % with experience of similar work |
|---|---|---|---|
| All grades | 104 | 32 | 31 |
| Grade 7 | 53 | 19 | 36 |
| HEO | 22 | 8 | 36 |
| SEO | 14 | 3 | 21 |
| HEO(D) | 15 | 2 | 13 |

*Source*: Compiled from interviews (see Appendix).

come back to haunt you. [Yet] there is a big difference between this area and the ones I have covered in the past. This is different, the customers are the pensions industry, investment organizations, and such like. There is a different learning curve—to other areas I have worked in. This is different. First it is very interesting and second the area takes very much longer to learn about. When I was doing international work...I was in a section with no legislative issues.

Those classed as having had 'previous experience' include those who work in bill teams, producing legislation, who have worked in bill teams before even if the bill was in a completely different area. If we were to have a more stringent definition of specialization, equating it with subject specialization, and were to define as 'specialists' only those officials with years of experience working in a specific functional area of public policy, we would be hard-pressed to find more than a dozen from our sample of 128.

The unusual character of subject specialization was reflected in the comment of the person serving third longest (four years) in the same post and in other posts in the same area for longer:

I am about to go on secondment to an area outside [this one]. My boss looked askance at someone who has been in [this area] for eighteen years, so he is sending me on secondment somewhere else.

Subject specialization is neither generally encouraged nor frequently developed. Even on the rare occasions when such specialization is claimed, it is not a particularly narrow specialism. One Grade 7 commented of his job:

There is an ethos in the civil service that civil servants should move frequently, and I'm not like that. I have an interest in work on the environment and we have a small team that I like and it is a good one.

Yet he indicated that he construed his interest in the environment broadly: while his current work was about sustainability, he added: 'I am interested in public health. If I were not in this area I would have liked to have gone to food or vaccines.' Another subject 'specialist' said:

I have been in this area six or seven years. I am an expert on Northern Ireland. I got posted in this job a year ago. I was working on Northern Ireland, but was a grade lower and I was promoted into this job. I am leaving the job in autumn. They asked me to stay for the spending review. Now that is done I can look for something else. It was a nice way in at the higher level—doing something you were expert at.... I will move on in autumn. I am interested in moving away from spending. I'll go on a level transfer. I am interested in the EU side. I have always had an interest in that.

## Skills and improvised expertise

No officials identified themselves as lacking the ability to do their jobs. Where they did not have the subject expertise initially, most expressed confidence that they could pick it up. One striking case of this tendency can be seen in the comments of an official, at the time an HEO (nine grades from the top of the civil service), who was asked to write some regulations for a major and reasonably high-profile government agency:

The Grade 6 came to us and asked us to do the regs [regulations]. We, Sue and I, had never done regulations or policy work before and we were told 'you're doing it'. All I had was an [HND in] Public Administration from ... [the] 1960s. I knew nothing about them. We spoke to people who had been involved in them. We got the name of the departmental solicitor and spoke to him. Sue's uncle is an MP and he helped. He sent us a load of material about the process of passing regulations in parliament.... I was temporarily promoted from HEO to SEO to do the job, my EO was temporarily promoted to HEO. We [were] working directly to a Grade 6 with no other support.

Not only did they write the regulations but they also dealt with much of the aftermath. One part of it was dealing with a possible legal challenge:

When we did the regulations the [major interest group] threatened to take them to judicial review. Sue and I thought, 'they're right' and the lawyer said so too. I wrote the response which I sent to [the Cabinet minister] who sent it out in his name. I wrote the thing. I don't think I'm paid enough money to do this sort of thing. . . . Anyway we got personal letters from the Grade 3 and Grade 2 congratulating us on our work. . . . I showed my mother the letter [the prominent Cabinet minister] wrote and told her that I [really] wrote it, but he just put his name to it. She did not believe it—'get away with you' she said.

It is not, then, surprising that the kinds of skill that respondents tended to mention when they were talking about the qualities needed to do their jobs hardly ever involved technical experience or subject knowledge. One high-flyer responsible for an important set of clauses in a major piece of legislation answered in response to the question of whether she was qualified to deal with the technical legal issues involved:

I had to familiarize myself with insolvency law. Lots of times this was through talking to colleagues who taught me a lot. Sometimes I'd look things up in a text book, but I'd never read a book cover to cover, just look at small sections covering the relevant bit of law I was interested in. We also have a bill team lawyer and I'd go to him. But mostly I learned from colleagues who would explain it to me.

Similar questions to other respondents about the types of skills one needed to do apparently technical work elicited answers that highlighted the importance of variants on being 'quick on the uptake'.

A Grade 5 official, commenting on some of the people working in his bill team who had no previous experience or knowledge of the substantive issues covered by the legislation, stated that this was not important since 'the fast streamers, and we had some who were at the upper range of ability, had the capability to run with the area very quickly'. 'Transferable skills', in the sense of having a capacity to turn one's hand to almost any type of policy work, is perhaps a more technical-sounding term to cover this view of the requirements of policy officials:

Policy work requires a bigger range of skills. [My old job] doing government accounts did not really give you any transferable skills. Here [in DEFRA] I could be an expert in rural policy but could just as easily go off to the Department of Transport or the DTI. [*Interviewer: So you could move out of DEFRA?*] Oh yes, that is quite possible. It would not be a problem if I wanted to leave.

Many stressed interpersonal skills:

The sort of skills you need in this job? You need to be able to get on with people, being able to see what is in the issue for them and being sensitive to what they want. You need to hold your own line. You need to be fairly *confident*—to stand up in meetings with translators and all the works of an international meeting can be intimidating. You have to be able to speak up. To be clear and confident.

Another stressed her blend of general ability to understand things, some technical skill, and the knowledge of whom to contact for further advice. She was working on the EU budget, and we asked, given that she had just outlined some fairly technical issues, how she developed that sort of expertise:

I had been in MAFF and DEFRA for ten years. I was in the economics side of MAFF, and I used to provide the analysis for these issues, so I like to think I am an intelligent consumer of their advice. The structure of the department has not changed all that much. I know the team and can call them up.

Technical knowledge was in some cases regarded as a handicap with policy work. An SEO who represented her department on an international working group argued:

I'm a generalist, many of the people at these meetings are researchers. Not sure whether they are contractors or what, but many of them are university-based. France, Germany, and New Zealand tend to send along civil servants, the rest are largely specialist experts. That can be problematic because they don't always think about what is useful for policymaking. The Swiss person might go on about multilevel sampling and all that, and leave us all behind. Other policy civil servants I speak to there also feel the same. The working group should be policy-based, and researchers kept off.

Where knowledge of the policy world was deemed important, it was more likely to be knowledge of the process rather than the substantive area. While bill teams writing legislation were more likely to include people with experience in the substantive area of policy than those working in other types of jobs, a couple of bill teams studied had large numbers of newcomers in the policy area. One official commented on the fact that she was the only member of the team with previous experience of bill work and that this qualified her as an authority on legislation:

I did a degree in Geography. . . . I have been in the DoH since the start. I worked . . . as a member of [a bill team on a prominent bill some years before]. When we started the legislation I was the only one with any experience on a bill. People would come and ask me about bills. It was scary.

Another graduate identified his area of policy as technical, but stressed the need for learning more about the policy processes and procedures rather than the technical issues, which could be more easily assimilated:

I got promoted to the job I do at the moment. I am managing the transposition of an EU Directive [on a controversial environmental safety issue], and I had to learn particularly about secondary and EU legislation to do it. It is an excellent job for an HEO to have . . . very difficult technically . . . and complicated from the legal point of view. It gets even more complicated because of the high level of political interest in [this topic] in Europe. European law is bad enough even if the thing is straightforward— but it can get really complicated when there's a lot of politics involved too.

Balancing the development of a range of process skills against narrow 'specialism' can also be difficult. A Grade 7 argued that bill team work 'gets you so far, but does not get you to the top. To have done one bill is good, but to do them all the time . . . I think there is an Oscar Wilde quote about that'. Another Grade 7 official believed he had moved around rather too much for his own good:

I like to move from job to job but that means that I don't have all that much credibility, not only among colleagues, but also to specialists in the field. I feel I need to develop a specialism.

Yet a graduate pointed to the slightly shifting fortunes of the subject specialist in his department. Although the sentiments were rare, his comments could reflect the rather mixed, or changing, messages that are stressed at different periods:

[*Interviewer: Do you specialize in something in your career?*] When I first joined MoD twelve years ago there was no specialism in the Department, unless you were a scientist. If you were in the administrative stream you were considered capable of doing anything. Since then things have come in cycles. They seemed to want specialism and competency for finances, handling contracts etc., so there was a move to encourage people to stay in a specialism. This was reinforced when central personnel management was done away with. It meant that as personnel was managed in segments it is harder to move across segments. Now they seem to be encouraging people to have a wider range of skills, so you are encouraged to have a broad range of experiences if you want to go on to be a Principal [Grade 7]. You have to demonstrate competencies across a range of areas, so you have to be posted across a range of areas. Throughout my career I've dodged this specialism. I've done finance, personnel, and several policy jobs and do not consider myself specialist and would avoid this.

An official, who had had experience working in the Cabinet Office as well as other departments, and was about to leave the civil service, suggested that there were signs of change in the old system, which typically rewarded the sparky person rather than someone accomplished or experienced in any particular area, but for the moment it remained dominant:

People at the top are rewarded and get on for being clever, academically bright, and going through jobs like private office and the Cabinet Office where you get lots of chances to show how clever you are, how you can hold your own with ministers and all sorts of clever people in verbal jousting. These kind of senior executives are congenitally incapable of managing in another way. This is a real problem.

What is emphasized in policy jobs is essentially the ability to pick things up—to pick up the variety of cues that exist to help shape decisions and actions while doing policy work. In Chapter 5 we will explore further the precise cues that help guide policy.

## Conclusions

Our middle-level officials are a diverse bunch. The policy bureaucracy is populated with people of rather different kinds—people passing through on their way to jobs in the higher civil service and people who will finish their civil service careers at the middle level. In what sense are our middle-level officials 'experts'? Not in their educational qualifications. Although many, but not all, have degrees, few have degrees or qualifications that equip them to do their current jobs. They are not experts because they stay in the same jobs for a long time or spend large parts of their careers concentrating on working in any one particular area of public policy. Some do so, but they are exceptions to the general rule that people are moved between jobs fairly rapidly, and generally appointed to jobs in which they have no direct experience. As Kingsley (1944: 175) argued over sixty years ago, 'the expert in the civil service is . . . regarded without enthusiasm by his administrative colleagues'.[19]

The consequence of this lack of subject specialization will be examined in our overall conclusions, but the patterns of career development do underline the transience of technical expertise. When an official who had spent months working on a single piece of legislation was asked if she looked at how the legislation was working now that it had been in force for a couple of years, she answered: 'I am interested but you have to move on to the next thing. Someone else is the expert on that now—you lose expertise. I am interested, but not in a profound way. It is someone else's patch.' Officials do not perceive themselves to be particularly disadvantaged by moving on frequently and having jobs covering topics with which they are largely unfamiliar. As one fast streamer commented: 'I can make judgements about the issues even though I don't really know the issue areas they are dealing with. A good submission [i.e. a well argued memorandum setting out the arguments] will allow you to do that.'

This chapter has not answered the question of the basis of the expertise of officials except partially in negative terms, by saying in what senses they are not experts. To be in a position to answer this question we need to leave the discussion about the personal skills and experiences of our middle-ranking officials and look at the nature of policy work. When we understand what policy bureaucrats do, and the range of tasks they undertake, we can describe more effectively where they acquire the skills to do them. A description of different kinds of 'policy work' is the task of Chapter 3.

# 3

# Policy Work

The policy bureaucrats in the middle ranks of the civil service work on policy. But what is 'policy work'? Civil servants regularly describe themselves as doing 'policy work' or having a 'policy job', but what do they mean? Surely it cannot mean they actually *make* policy? After all, elected politicians are supposed to *make* policy. While some might be convinced that civil servants may under some circumstances have taken over this policymaking role, it surely could not be those people much lower down who only had, at best, walk-on parts in the tragedies and dramas of Whitehall and Westminster (a stage now extended to more distant outposts such as Leeds, Newcastle, Edinburgh, and Cardiff). Our scepticism would be justified only if policymaking were a single act of creation. While policymaking is undoubtedly creative, involving setting out new (or at least revised) ways of doing things as well as packaging and presenting them, it is not a single act but a continuous (and often iterative) process. Just as government in general combines political and bureaucratic activities, so too does policymaking.

If policy work is not actually 'making policy' in the sense of making an authoritative decision such as passing a law or changing a budget, to understand what policy bureaucracies do we must ask those who do most of the policy work, those in the middle grades, what they do. Officials almost invariably perceive policy work to be different from other forms of civil service work, and this perception is presented in the next section. While the range of jobs that policy civil servants do appears immense, their work can nevertheless be grouped into three broad categories. These categories are important as a means of understanding the type of work that policy officials do, and they are also important as a basis for setting out the ways in which policymaking as a bureaucratic activity can shape the overall result of the policy-making process. This chapter sets out how middle-ranking officials go about their policy work and the types of decisions they have to make. The question of whether these activities and decisions are essentially subordinate to, or narrowly circumscribed by, previous 'strategic' decisions about policy taken by politicians and senior officials is discussed in Chapter 4.

## Views of policy work

Middle-grade civil servants are clear about what a 'policy job' is. Almost without exception they described their careers as movement into a policy job. While interviews did not concentrate on semantic issues, where respondents drew distinctions between other types of job—most frequently 'casework', 'management', 'operations', and 'implementation' (with which some also combined their current policy jobs)—they tended to argue that policy work involved thinking about, or developing, programmes. They stressed creativity. An official involved in making sure that government policy plans were 'delivered' saw this role as the less policy-oriented part of her job:

My team's role is to make sure it happens—we are about nagging, monitoring, and supporting. It depends on which department we are dealing with, which mix of these we use. Some departments are easier to deal with than others. I would not say we see a huge amount of the minister—not as much as I had in the last job I did. We are at the boring end of things. Yes, delivery is everything, but not something you need to go to the minister about. Most ministerial stuff goes up in correspondence, submissions, and the like. In the last job, a policy development job, I was meeting the minister a lot, weekly.

A Grade 7 in the Treasury described the amount of creativity as the 'meatiness' of the policy job:

Let me illustrate my role by talking about the job I did before (in HM Treasury), with responsibility for [a particular spending department]. There the head of the team was not paying too much attention and so I was doing more [than I do now]. I had a greater input into the Public Service Agreement structure [PSA—the system of performance targets that spending departments are expected to meet as a condition of receiving Treasury funds]. I was directly arguing with [the spending department] that some of the PSA targets they were putting up made no sense. I wrote one of the PSA targets myself, obviously in consultation with others. Nobody has the illusion that here I make policy, the only area I do it is where I see that senior people will look at it too. That previous job was policy-meaty.

An official in the MoD emphasized the apparent randomness of his influence:

You come here thinking that policy is about sitting round a table and deciding what you are going to do, but it tends to fall out of what goes on. It is funny how things become policy. Sometimes you put in a briefing and in the briefing there is a sentence or line saying 'this is one way of doing things' or several sentences outlining different ways. This gets mentioned at a meeting and gets support. The next thing you know is that this is now decided as 'policy'.

Contact with senior officials and politicians is an important part of policy work. An MoD official said:

One thing people like about a key policy job is that the chain of command is compacted. I get to speak to people other people of my grade don't usually get to speak to. I often talk to my two-star general grade and submit things to him that go to the Secretary of State.

However, this contact is not a defining characteristic of a policy job. Some forms of ministerial contact—simply providing briefings and information to politicians—are not generally regarded as 'policy work'. 'Feeding the beast', as one SEO put it, referring to providing information to politicians to help them in the political process by answering parliamentary questions or answering the queries of speech writers or press offices, is generally not of itself a policy job since several respondents who had done these jobs regarded them as pretty routine. Such work only becomes part of a generally more interesting policy job when linked with one's direct policy responsibility—involving some part in developing, running, or evaluating a programme or scheme. Speeches and briefings given to ministers by officials preparing new legislation are especially important since, according to the doctrine associated with the 1993 *Pepper* v. *Hart* case, what is said by a minister in Parliament during the legislative process can be used subsequently in court to help determine the meaning of the law (see Steyn 2001; Page 2003).

Most policy jobs brought involvement in several policies at any one time. The modal number of different policy issues within the responsibility of the respondents interviewed was three. What is described as a 'separate' job varies from one respondent to the next. Grade 7 officials generally mentioned their management tasks as well as their policy tasks, and policy tasks were seldom singular but combined with other tasks. Many officials interviewed served as heads of secretariats for consultative groups—whether internal government groups, such as HM Treasury Management Board, or involving outsiders, such as the Japan Electronic Business Association in the DTI. In addition to assessing risks associated with diseases of plants, a DEFRA Grade 7 official has to represent DEFRA at the relevant EU committee and develop policy on public consultations about agricultural issues. Sometimes the combination of tasks was unusual. One such combination included financial policy matters and responsibility for the consequences of a major national (non-financial) scandal, which 'was dumped on us as there was nowhere else'.

Moreover, as noted in Chapter 2, policy jobs tend to change once people come into them. One HEO in the DoH who had been in post less than a year found she was doing rather different work to that for which she was appointed:

I was recruited to look at the implementation side and the costings too. But the job changed from what I was recruited for since there are changes in what needs to be done. I now look at detailed policy issues. We have to go through the 1983 Mental Health Act section by section to see what needs to be changed in the light of the White Paper. I have responsibility for [a set of] clauses. One of the things I have is what happens when MPs are held under the legislation (they lose their seats after six months). Yes, this is a thing that I say to people to make it sound interesting. You may laugh but there is a serious issue at stake if you are trying to reduce the stigma of mental health. . . . [So] the job has shifted. Some of the people in the [group working with me] are new. The other Grade 7 has taken on the implementation stuff. I have taken on some additional parts. When I started it was half detailed policy and half implementation, but it has changed to more detailed policy. I have [also] taken on the part of the Act that relates to people in prison— dangerous offenders with mental health problems.

Although policy officials had no difficulty in describing themselves as such, the term describes a wide variety of jobs, as is clear from the brief descriptions of the handful of jobs we have outlined so far in this chapter. Are there any common features to these jobs apart from creativity and contact with politicians?

Before describing policy jobs it should be noted that policy jobs are not the sole jobs of policy officials. Many combine policy with non-policy work such as answering parliamentary questions, providing information to the press office, tending to some of the more routine aspects of running existing programmes, and, especially among Grade 7s, managing a team—a task that includes dealing with personnel issues. A handful of policy officials interviewed said that they spent more time on non-policy work than on policy work. However, we cannot offer precise figures on the allocation of time since a reliable estimate would have required a structured survey instrument offering a common definition of policy work. This may have been possible, but would have taken up a larger portion of our 20-minute interview time than could be justified by the focus of this research: this study is not primarily concerned with how officials spend their working time, but with how they do their policy work. Thus we need to know what policy work is.

## The forms of policy work

While the range of policy jobs was as diverse as the range of policy issues that governments have to deal with, it was possible to distinguish between three types of policy job on the basis of the type of output they produce. A *production* policy job produces some form of draft, statement, or document. It is concerned with a one-off task, usually with a written document, or a set of them, as its final product. A *maintenance* policy job involves tending a particular regime or set of institutions—making or recommending day-to-day decisions about how a particular scheme or set of institutions should be handled. While a production job generally finishes once the document it usually produces has been written, maintenance jobs have no end point. If you are responsible for a particular set of policies, you stay with it until the policy finishes or you move to another job. A *service* policy job involves giving advice or other assistance to an individual or a body, usually on a continual basis. We illustrate further each of these three types of policy jobs.

## Production

The documents that arise from production policy work can be of a variety of sorts. Several of our respondents were part of a bill team given the task of producing and shepherding legislation through parliament. The role of bill teams has been discussed in Chapter 2 and in greater detail elsewhere (Page 2003). The typical bill team is a group of civil servants headed by a Grade 7, with the size depending on the complexity of the proposed legislation. One Grade 7 official described how she was for the most part a 'one-person bill team' in her previous job:

A Grade 3 came and asked me if I wanted to do a bill, and I worked to a Grade 5 in London where I did . . . [an NHS finance bill]. This was a brilliant job. It was a medium-sized bill. I started off on my own and then got an HEO to help.

Whereas, the Enterprise Bill in the DTI was a much larger affair with over forty officials and, rather unusually, overseen by three Grade 5s (one is usual). Whether big or small, the policy work of a bill team is the same—to develop policy guidelines into legislative clauses. The process is indirect—bill teams pass on the policy guidance to the departmental solicitors, who write instructions that are passed on to the barristers who write the legislation: Parliamentary Counsel employed in the Office of Parliamentary Counsel. Bill teams have a role to play in taking a bill through Parliament, where one of the major policy roles is to ensure that amendments are handled properly—that ministers are briefed and advised whether to accept them, how to respond to them if they are not directly accepted, and how they should be drafted in the event that they are accepted.

Regulation writing, usually through a Statutory Instrument ('doing the regs'), is also a common task for officials. Statutory Instruments (see Page 2001) arise from a variety of circumstances. Recently passed Acts of Parliament often require such regulations to set them in force, and sometimes secondary legislation will be needed to deal with issues the government did not for some reason resolve as the bill was passing through—possibly because of lack of time or because the issue involved was too contentious. An HEO(D) who had been working on a bill team described her work thus:

On the bill now my role is coming to an end. We are looking beyond the bill to what we are going to consult on. We are thinking of regulations coming on the back of the bill. Large chunks of the bill give outline—the details are in the regs and we're going to consult on the details in all the regs. You get to know what needs to be done through the long process of the bill. When you are developing it you think 'there is a problem here' or you get it talking to stakeholders in developing the legislation and you pull together ideas.

Statutory Instruments are also the way EU directives are put into UK law. We came across an HEO who was writing Statutory Instruments in a contentious food-related issue: 'I came in after the directive had been negotiated. My boss, the Grade 7, was involved in the negotiations, and I came in after it had gone through the EU. I had to write the regulation implementing it.'

Regulation writing is often taken in the stride of a longer-standing service or maintenance job. One official, responsible for statutory maternity pay, had to think about helping write new primary legislation, regulations, as well as guidance as part of her (normal) maintenance job:

My main job is looking after statutory maternity pay and allowances. I will have responsibility for legislation which surrounds these and take forward the legislation that comes from the government's plans in this area. I have to work closely with DTI and Inland Revenue on this. My main task at the moment is to make sure changes in maternity are carried forward as part of the [Employment] Bill and to look after the regulations needed after. ... As the bill is passing through Parliament (it is in the Lords Committee at the moment), a colleague in the section and I have been responsible for instructing solicitors and looking at the effects of amendments put forward and briefings for ministers. ... Also, at the same time I have written detailed instructions for regulations. There are two sets—one set won't involve the SSAC [the Social Security Advisory Committee, which has statutory rights of consultation on some social security legislation] as they come direct from primary legislation, the other set has bits that will have to go to SSAC.

The procedures to be followed in writing a regulation tend to be drafting 'policy instructions' to departmental solicitors, ensuring that the resulting draft does what you want it to do, for some Statutory Instruments sending out some for public consultation, and for all of them securing ministerial approval (for more details see Page 2001).

White Papers outlining the possibility of legislation also provide a focus for project work. One official interviewed was involved in outlining the future of the fire services—especially sensitive because at that time firefighters were in a long-standing and somewhat bitter industrial dispute with their employers and, indirectly, the government. As a Grade 7 he was in the early stages of the White Paper, in a team which involved a Grade 3 and an SEO. His job was not to produce one document but several others too—since he was at an initial stage at the time of interview: 'There is an expectation that I will put a submission to ministers next week. That will contain a project plan, a communication strategy and a consultation process'. Another official was developing a White Paper on a particular part of the energy industry:

I am currently working on the White Paper which should end up with a bill on reform [in the sector]. I am in a team that will turn into a legislative team, but we have not got a bill or a slot yet [i.e. there is no legislation being drafted and there is no guarantee yet that space will be found in the parliamentary timetable to legislate in this area]. There are eight of us in the team, the head is SCS Grade 5....I have been given specific policy issue areas. I was not part of the initial dividing up, so I don't really know how it came about. My responsibility is to look after some of the chapters of the White Paper. The team agreed an outline of what should be in my part before I came. There are different chapters covering the structure, organization, constitution, and funding [of a new regulatory body we are planning to set up]. I have the constitution, whether it should be a non-departmental public body or agency.

White Paper work was mentioned by several of our respondents as 'good to do' as it could have many of the advantages of bill work— 'senior exposure' and the ability to show creativity and initiative.

In addition many other projects produce draft policy statements or proposals that are not part of the legislative process. Two officials interviewed in the ODPM were responsible for helping produce the new system for allocating central government grants to local authorities. They had rather different roles in the process: one had to go through the emerging allocation formula and identify anomalies and political problems arising from it (including disproportionate or undesired effects of the change to the new system); and the other, a different function.

I play two roles. I am a statistician and I lead the data team that the formula runs on. My other role is the policy lead for fire [services] element of the formula. For working out the new formula I gave advice on indicators to the policy leads [i.e. people responsible for other specific components of the grant]. [Advice] about the suitability and availability of data. [*Interviewer: So you were providing advice to different clients in other parts of your Branch, how did this work? Did they ask you what sorts of indicators are good for this or that purpose?*] Not exactly. There is a broad spectrum of indicators around and people tend to be aware of them—for example data on income support. There, my task is to tell about availability and such like. Then there are broader questions—trying to find an indicator of social class for the personal social services (PSS) formula. It had been shown by research projects that this was a driver of PSS costs. The standard measures were based on the 1991 census and my advice was sought. I actually pinpointed the problem saying that the 1991 census was out of date and the 2001 census does not have it in it. And I tried to find a replacement—I did [find one] based on the Labour Force Survey.

Several of the Treasury officials were involved in monitoring spending in government departments, and, while part of their job is generally defined as maintenance as they have to keep an ongoing watch on their departments, the biennial spending review provides the rhythm to this job and every other year (officials in the Treasury were interviewed in the off year after the spending round had been completed) their maintenance work is eclipsed by project work marked by the production of a budget at the end and, even more project-like, a 'settlement letter'.

Writing the settlement letter is the key task. Do you know about settlement letters? Well the Public Service Agreement [the performance targets set by the Treasury for the department] is published and the amount of money is also published. But the settlement letter is confidential. It goes from the Chief Secretary to the spending minister. It contains some stock phrases. It always says, even if it's not an 'excellent' settlement, 'We have agreed an excellent settlement' and goes on to explain the totals for the three years, the breakdown between capital and current spending, the breakdown of administrative spending, all things which are public knowledge. It goes on to say 'we require you to do such and such a thing'—a review of how something is done, perhaps, with the implication that we did not think this worked very efficiently. In the longer term the minister will be expected to have a business plan. This is a very useful document from the Treasury's point of view as a way of getting things changed. . . . The document has the potential to be frank and candid—setting out the fiscal realities. It is personally presented. The Chancellor will invite the spending minister in, with his permanent secretary, over a whisky and hand him the letter: 'Here's your settlement letter, let's go through it.' He won't know what is in it until after he has spoken to his officials. They have a parallel copy, and the head of the spending team will talk to the head of finance in the relevant department at the same time. . . . I draft the letter. It is in draft for five weeks, with any number of drafts going backwards and forwards. There are some cross-cutting bits in many of the letters—scientific research has to go up. Managing the cross-cutting issues will generate extra length. The . . . letter [I was responsible for] was thirty pages long.

*Papers* that set out options and discuss strategies for developing policy are another kind of project work. One SEO had been charged to write a paper on childcare:

It is about proposals for managing an informal childcare pilot. I have been putting forward a paper for the design appraisal. This was started by someone in Leeds at a lower grade. The Grade 7 was away, I am pulling together the presentation and fleshing it out. It is about paying relatives instead of childminders.

This project was unusual since it was both outside his own area of responsibility and there was also some uncertainty over whether his department was even responsible for the task.

The proposals from [the main department responsible] have not persuaded [the minister in this department] they would work. They would allow temporary informal carer payments as long as the person becomes a childminder. That is why [the minister] wanted the department to do it. This occupied me Friday and yesterday. This is peculiar because childcare is not me. The responsibility lies in [another part of the department]. Those people are all involved in [another big project] and so we have got it.

Another official was charged with simplifying a wide range of schemes offered by the department:

We are a change programme. The [department] offers 180 different schemes [in this particular area] . . . and our job is to consolidate them to less than 20 and impose a strategy. The schemes are devolved and it is a bit of a mess. The scheme manager operates independently, and we are trying to create a system to make the schemes complement each other. This involves (*a*) finding out what is going on; this is no mean feat—there is lots going on and we did not know before now what it was, but we probably know now; and (*b*) devising a structure—not sure what it is now but it will turn into a centralized structure. It will own the strategy. We own the change and give it on to be managed, but the strategy will be ours and we will control it.

In this specific case the output of the work would be a set of proposals that would remain unpublished.

Production work often involves dealing with interest groups and other organizations outside government. When a late change to a major crime-related measure was being drafted, the Grade 7 concerned said: 'we had to get agreement very quickly with police, NCIS [The National Criminal Intelligence Service], the banking community, and the Treasury to be able to instruct the lawyer what we wanted to do.' An official drafting a consultation document outlining options for development of a major public service consulted relevant groups to help decide the range of issues the document should cover:

We have done the inventory of things to be included in the [discussion document], the range of topics. . . . For the meeting with [the main organization representing staff involved], I will write a note saying 'this is what we propose to cover'. We invite them to put on the table what they want to raise—I have taken this approach with all stakeholders.

Moreover, the relationship is not always simply a matter of listening to what the group has to say. Officials can develop collaborative relationships with them. An official helping draw up plans for the development of a historic site had to consult one of the statutory (non-government) advisory organizations:

[The organization] has a statutory advisory role. The thing I did was to encourage [it] . . . to frame [its] comments in such a way that it could be clear and so that you can deconstruct the debate. That sounds like French existentialism. I asked them to separate [two distinct technical issues involved in the proposal]. We did not want the situation at the public inquiry where people were [conflating the two]. [The organization] . . . came out and had its options report—they gave clear advice that [one of the options] is not acceptable. . . . This made it easier to give advice to ministers. I could say that in view of the advice from [the organization] we could not put money into something different from that which was clearly approved by the statutory advisers.

On one occasion an official sought to dissuade a major interest group from encouraging those who supported its aims to break the law—he had to point out that the organization's lawyers were wrong in believing that they had found a legal loophole. Yet contact with groups is not limited to production work, it can also be an important part of maintenance and service work.

Production work—working on some kind of project such as a bill, White Paper, regulations, or some other distinct policy initiative—is the form of policy work that conforms most closely to conventional understandings of policymaking. Instead of 'advising' ministers on particular policy initiatives—the common characterization of how civil servants help shape policy initiatives (see Dowding 1995)—with project work officials have direct responsibility for developing specific aspects of policy. Yet it is not the only way in which they influence policy.

## Maintenance

Maintenance entails tending a particular set of arrangements governing particular policies. While the person involved might or might not have been involved in setting up the regime, maintenance work is all about running it. A DEFRA Grade 7 is charged with monitoring research on plant diseases and securing the necessary regulations to deal with them:

What [do] we do? I deal with exclusion of organisms.... A lot of my work is associated with risk assessment and the selection of the risk management option. The scientific side of the risk assessment is done by the laboratory, the selection of the risk management and consultations with stakeholders is done by me.... We have a different policy for every [plant] pest. There are 300 pests in the Plant Health Directive (EU Directive 2000/29) and there are thousands that are not listed. For each organism we need to decide what to do: whether to do nothing, exclude it, or eradicate it.... When we know what our policy is, we have to negotiate it with Brussels. The policy might be that it should be listed as an organism, but the next stage is to convince the members of the Plant Standing Committee in Brussels.

Another classical maintenance policy job is that of a Treasury official who helps monitor defence spending:

The MoD had a huge delegation [of financial authority] from HM Treasury. It is able to approve its own projects up to around £400 million. It is not actually a specific figure, but [covers] a significant new project, so big money. A new project, a new aircraft or ship, something contentious or novel or international requires Treasury approval. So we advise on big things. We are in day-to-day business with the MoD on these issues. We help them with the formulation of the project. We don't want the Secretary of State to write to the Chief Secretary to the Treasury only for him to say 'no'. We make sure that the concerns that many programmes face when they go forward are addressed at the working stage.

As noted above, some of the Treasury officials interviewed had a kind of production role—that of producing every two years the budgeting documents arising from the spending review. They had an additional maintenance role, as their jobs involve continuous monitoring of government departments in the 'off' year of the biennial spending review process. One, when asked about the 'off' year, replied: 'Between reviews? Departments will be after extra money for this and extra for that.' His job was to scrutinize such requests. Another argued that he had a general watching brief on 'Connexions', a young people's career and educational advisory service:

Much of my work is on the spending review. In the lull year my job is very much to look at policy being developed in my area of responsibility. Is Connexions meeting our objectives? Looking at evaluation evidence on the education maintenance allowance to see if we should roll it out nationally (which we have done), looking at the performance of further education, and so on. The spending review comes along and you carry on doing the old [monitoring] job and add the spending review on top.

Making sure that other departments and organizations stick to the script of what has been agreed is a common maintenance task. An official in the ODPM is responsible for 'Local Public Service Agreements'. Local PSAs were pseudo-contracts between the government departments and individual local authorities to meet agreed performance targets. If these targets were met, the idea is that local authorities receive a financial reward. A Grade 7 argued:

My job has two bits. I spend part of the time dealing with specific regulations. The detailed negotiations are done with other departments—DEFRA on waste targets, DfES on education, and so on. I am the one who pulls it together and makes sure that departments don't agree to things that are not in the spirit of PSAs.

There were several officials charged with making sure that policies ran according to agreed principles:

I am in local government modernization—it is about the devolution of power and responsibility to local government. My particular bit is the coordination of performance agreements and regulatory control mechanisms. It is an attempt to counter the wave of centralizing controls that we have had since the mid 1980s—both in finance (getting rid of ring-fencing and other things), which is not my beef, and other areas (which are).

Similarly, several officials interviewed had the task of trying to make sure that ministerial or Cabinet-level decisions were adhered to in the day-to-day running of government. One official in DEFRA was responsible for implementing 'rural proofing':

All policy should be examined to see if there is a rural element that affects the policy, or if the policy needs to be altered in some way for the way it can work in a rural area. . . . If a policy relies on lots of different service outlets—there are fewer outlets in rural areas such as GP surgeries and shops—that won't work in rural areas. They need to modify them so they can work. . . . Rural proofing is about picking up an issue where the rural dimension has not been considered. So the idea is that where the department manages to incorporate the rural dimension we don't have anything to do. So if we are successful in getting people to think about the rural dimension, we could do ourselves out of a job. . . . I look after that issue as a policy development across Whitehall. It was introduced in a White paper in 2000 and DEFRA was the lead department in developing a new strategy for rural proofing. We and the Countryside Agency [took the lead].

The Social Exclusion Unit (SEU), a body that develops anti-poverty policies and is based now in the ODPM (formerly in the Cabinet Office), has a Grade 7 looking at implementation issues. Many of the SEU reports recommend action in one or more other departments, so ensuring implementation is a key part of SEU activity:

The implementation set-up followed an SEU external review in 1999–2000 which highlighted a weakness: there was no specific team to ensure that things in the [SEU] reports happened. The team was set up in 2000. . . . A lot of our job is reactive. It depends on what departments are doing on an issue. We are trying to build in proactivity. For each report we have a paper that sets out our goals, progress on implementation, issues that have not happened, and an action plan for what we do. We set out priorities.

There are similar jobs in other departments which seek to make sure that cross-departmental priorities, such as the development of waste management schemes, are carried out.

Running 'evaluations' of programmes is a frequent maintenance task. Often these evaluations are contracted out to universities or consultants. A DfES official spoke of his work in the use of digital television to deliver education

We had about sixty schools in the scheme. We did it together with Granada and the BBC. . . . It was a pilot simulating digital television teaching for GCSE in Maths, Science, and History with half a term's worth of materials. . . . We managed the contracts with the providers—tender, assessment, negotiation (we used specialists, of course, such as lawyers and accountants to help us do that). BECTA [British Educational Communications and Technology Agency] advised us on this and SCREE [Scottish Council for Research in Education Evaluation] did the evaluation. We do the outside evaluation then decide what to do.

Maintenance work is not simply a matter of delivery or implementation. It is also policy work and, given the general bias against the development of subject specialization, is arguably the kind of work in which it is possible for officials to gain greatest familiarity with a particular issue, even though they may be dealing with it for only a few years before they move on.

## Service

Service in a general sense is something all civil servants provide. In the specific sense used here, service work is a matter of offering knowledge and skills to others who produce policies. Offering advice to a minister is the clearest version of service work. Many of the MoD officials interviewed were concerned primarily with providing advice on what the UK line should be on relations with other countries and in dealing with bodies such as NATO. A Grade 7 stated:

> The main output of the job is advising ministers and senior military officers on the Balkans. There is also a technical side of organizing our people in the Balkans. For example, we are trying to sort out three posts for military officers to go to Bosnia, Kosovo, and Macedonia, priming people to go, briefing and defining their role. There are lots of single posts around.

Another pointed out that the service-type job was not the most interesting of policy jobs:

> I have been in the job a year. This is my first job in the policy area. I am quite surprised that a lot of what I had thought would be a policy job was like secretariat work—briefing for events, developing lines to be taken for ministers, attaching background to reports for people on visits. A lot is similar to non-policy jobs I have done. Sometimes I think I was suckered into it. You're told it is great doing 'policy' but you are doing the same old briefing.

Advising and briefing is a common part of many officials' jobs, even though much of their time is concerned with production or maintenance jobs. Treasury officials who monitor the spending of government departments have to brief the Chief Secretary and even the Chancellor in their dealings with spending ministries. A Grade 7 described his experiences in the last spending round:

> I prepare the briefings for the meetings with the Secretary of State [in the spending department] and I go along with the head of the team when we put them up for the Chief Secretary to the Treasury and we need to speak to them [i.e. elaborate on the briefings]. Yes I go along to the bilaterals [with the spending department] too. You'll have the Chief Sec[retary] to the Treasury, the [Secretary of State for the spending department], a Cabinet Office presence from Gus McDonald and we all hear what the Secretary of State has to say. The Chief Secretary will have been briefed on

how to conduct the meeting. There will be an exchange of differences rather than of view. The overall thrust of policy is agreed and the delivery of policy is left for us to pick up after. I've done lots of spending reviews, and it has never really been all that different. . . . [In this one the spending department's minister insisted on seeing the Chancellor.] I had to brief the Chancellor. [Chancellor Gordon] Brown . . . is very good. He just looks at the briefing, picks up a couple of points, and runs with those.

An HEO(D) working in a permanent secretary's private office had a distinctive advisory role:

Another role unique to me as the Perm[anent] Sec[retary]'s private secretary in this department is advising on propriety. Ministers have private interests that could lead to perceptions of conflict of interests. Advice comes from the permanent secretary to deal with this, but I in fact do it.

A Grade 7 distinguished his advisory work from his policy job considering it more like 'casework'—the job was to make decisions in some cases in the name of the Home Secretary, and in more sensitive cases advise the Home Secretary, who makes the decision himself, about how mentally disordered offenders should be handled in the mental health system.

You tend to tell the minister in advance if there is any development in sensitive cases such as a mass killer whom they want to move from a high- to medium-security establishment. But in sensitive cases you usually put the proposal to the minister for agreement.

A classic service job is serving in the private office of a minister or a permanent secretary. Most junior ministerial offices are run by fast streamers, and fast streamers also dominated in the Secretary of State private offices in which we interviewed. Typically a private office for a junior minister or permanent secretary will consist of a diary secretary, a correspondence manager at a junior level (usually EO), and a private secretary, usually with a grade equivalent to an SEO, although this position is often filled by a fast-stream civil servant at HEO(D). The private secretary may have one or two assistants, generally at HEO level. For a Cabinet minister running a large ministry, private office is likely to be larger. One private office official described the set-up thus:

In the office we have a PPS (at Grade 5), a Grade 7 (me), two HEOs (personal secretaries), and two diary secretaries (EOs), and there is a whole raft of correspondence people upstairs.

The job involves deciding which of all the correspondence coming through to private office the minister needs to see. A Grade 7 in the office of a senior Cabinet minister described the process:

We decide what he needs to see and what he does not need to see. We also help him to get through the material. As you know, he is not the sort of person who is going to sit down and read through twenty pages of a document. I put a compliments slip on the front with what is in it and explain things.... Then we get his reaction and also make sure that his wishes are carried out and make sure he is brought into the decision-making process at the right time.

There is not only the matter of whether the minister needs to see something but also how urgent it is. 'The question is does she need to do something about this at all, and if so, is it today or this week?' Another official made a distinction between the types of material that come into private office:

There are three categories of things that come up: (i) 'we need a decision on this, please, minister'; (ii) 'minister, we think you need to know about this'; and (iii) a broad swathe of things [the minister does not need to see]. We are copied into a whole lot of correspondence.

Officials in private office not only serve their minister, they also answer queries from officials throughout the department. Some of the correspondence will be from officials asking for a ministerial decision or comment.

I need to take care that everything that goes to the minister has what he needs to know with it. And once the minister has agreed to something sometimes you have to go back and explain what the minister has said. Often it is very basic, 'the minister has noted what you have said and is content for you to carry on along the lines you suggest', other times it is more complicated and he will ask questions and ask for additional stuff to be actioned—briefings, press releases, and such like.

Moreover, officials in other parts of the department, sometimes senior officials, approach middle-ranking officials about the timing of their approach to the minister, how the minister is likely to respond to a proposal, and even the best way to frame an approach to the minister. As one commented:

I get phone calls all day asking whether a certain thing needs to go to the minister. And they ask me to give my thoughts on an issue—would she want to go to this [event]? Should I update her now on that?

Another described her work in this way.

Sometimes I am asked to give advice of my own—'is this something the minister will be relaxed about if asked or will he need convincing?' For example, if there is a PFI question,[20] I can say that the last three were stinkers, so the minister is likely to be skeptical.

This access to the minister and the insights into the minister's frame of mind puts officials in private office in a potentially powerful position. One private secretary commented:

It is better for people to have me happy to see them than not. I can be difficult if other people are difficult, and I can be difficult when I know that the minister wants me to be difficult. But I also have to remember that I am the one conduit between the department and the minister. My job is to make sure I am on good terms with officials. People learn quickly what they should do.

This power appears not to be used for self-aggrandizement. None of the officials interviewed suggested that private office and its officials stood between them and the minister. A Grade 7 who had, as a fast streamer, served in private office argued:

[Interviewer: Is there any resentment from other officials, perhaps senior, that private office controls access to the minister but is staffed by fast streamers?] No, there is no resentment, and no feeling of superiority. Everyone realizes they will not be in private office forever, so if you make enemies it will rebound on you.

In addition to advising ministers and acting as ministers' private secretaries, another common service job for middle-ranking officials is acting as head of the secretariat for a government-based body, perhaps an internal departmental body. An HEO(D) who headed the secretariat of his department's Management Board said:

I manage the formal agenda and advise on process issues. The Board meets twice a month and involves me commissioning papers and meeting the authors to coordinate and proof them. What sorts of documents? Two types: policy/strategy and business/management. Broadly the Board identifies issues they want to know more about or people in the [Department] want to know more about. Nuts and bolts reports on what is going on in management as well as broader things like Public Private Partnerships [a form of financing public projects which was politically sensitive at the time]. So that is my secretariat role.

Secretariat roles are not necessarily simply preparing agendas and shuffling paper. An official who worked on the secretariat to the Work and Parents Taskforce had to take an active role in the central purpose of the taskforce: to secure an agreement between employers' organizations and unions about the 'flexible working' arrangements to be included in the 2002 Employment Act:

What was key with this legislation is that the flexible working was the most contentious issue in the [Employment] Green Paper. The government did something smart by setting up a taskforce with [among others the representatives of the CBI and TUC] and forced all the parties to sit around a table together, expose their positions, and gain an understanding of the other party's claims. We got agreement on recommendations and this agreement gave the results of the Taskforce strength and credibility when it came to taking it through parliament and avoided any particularly nasty debates that might otherwise have arisen—they could say that the Taskforce had agreed this.

## Giving numbers

Policy work involves a range of different activities. We have presented it as falling into three groups. Real life is messier, as officials combine different sorts of work in any one job. For some, such as many working on a major bill team, there will be nothing else to work on; for others, writing a specific regulation or piece of guidance might be a normal part of maintaining a particular set of policies or servicing some particular body. If we assign our respondents to only one category of policy job, we would class fifty-seven (or 47 per cent of the 122 we could code) as project workers, forty-six (38 per cent) as maintenance workers, and nineteen (16 per cent) as service workers (Table 3.1).

Fast streamers (HEO(D)s), due to their frequent presence in private offices of ministers and permanent secretaries, were better represented among service workers (37 per cent) than other types of workers; Grade 6 and 7 officials were more numerous among the maintenance workers (61 per cent) than they were among other types of policy workers; and lower grades (HEOs and SEOs) were better represented among the production policy worker respondents than other types.

The figures in Table 3.1 cannot be extrapolated to offer any estimates of different types of policy worker in the civil service as a whole or of the grades that fill different roles. We expect that production workers have likely been overrepresented among our respondents because of our request to interview members of bill teams, and service workers are also possibly overestimated, as a couple of departments put forward as interview respondents larger numbers of HEO(D)s than we might have expected from a random sample. If true, and we have no real way of knowing, this overrepresentation of production and service jobs in our sample suggests a substantial underestimate of the maintenance work that goes on in the civil service. However, our central purpose in this study is not to quantify the incidence of different kinds of policy jobs, but rather to understand the character of policy work and how policy officials do it. There are, we believe, sufficient numbers in each category to have some confidence that we are presenting a fair picture of the range of policy work done by middle-ranking officials.

TABLE 3.1    Forms of policy work

| | Production (47% of respondents) | | Maintenance (38% of respondents) | | Service (16% of respondents) | |
|---|---|---|---|---|---|---|
| | No. | % | No. | % | No. | % |
| HEO(D) | 6 | 11 | 3 | 7 | 7 | 37 |
| Grade 6/7 | 23 | 40 | 28 | 61 | 9 | 47 |
| HEO/SEO | 23 | 40 | 15 | 33 | 3 | 16 |
| Unknown | 5 | 9 | 0 | 0 | 0 | 0 |
| Total | 57 | 100 | 46 | 100 | 19 | 100 |

*Source*: Compiled from interviews (see Appendix).

## Conclusions

It is not possible to tell how desirable policy jobs are on the basis of our interviews. Certainly many expressed their pleasure at having moved from a dreary old casework position or a job in the field. But since we did not expressly ask about job satisfaction, and since we spoke only to people in policy jobs, we cannot tell—those in other jobs might be just as happy doing what they are doing as our respondents appeared to be from the casual remarks they offered while describing their work. The conversations we had with our respondents, however, suggested they *believed* their jobs were preferable to other types of civil service job. One indicator of this belief came in the form of career movements indicated by our respondents. While we came across three who were on the verge of leaving the civil service, the destinations of those changing jobs within the civil service was overwhelmingly in the direction of taking on another policy job, and we came across none who hankered after a job in 'operations' or casework, with the exception of some London-based promotion aspirants and high-flyers who saw getting a job outside ministerial headquarters as a help to their careers, with every expectation of returning to a policy job in Whitehall.

The three broad categories of production, maintenance, and service offer a wide range of jobs. It is possible that other types of policy work were hidden from us because of the non-random sampling methods used, although the bias would have to have been extraordinarily large to be able to hide it in a sample of just 122—the number of valid cases here. But even within the categories we found, there are many different specific jobs. Serving a minister is different from serving, say, the Advisory Council on the Misuse of Drugs or a trade council, working on a bill is different from working on a budget, and having responsibility for Kosovo is not the same as responsibility for school examinations. One reason for distinguishing between the three types of work is that they offer a clearer way of describing, setting out, the sorts of work that policy officials do. Another reason for describing different types of policy work is that the kind of influence that policy work can have on the policy process is shaped by the type of work: officials in different kinds of work also make different types of choices. In Chapter 4 we will look at the types of decisions and issues that officials have to face in these types of work.

# 4

# More than Embellishment and Detail: The Impact of Policy Work

## Embellishing strategic policy decisions?

Much policy work, whether service, maintenance, or even project work, is conducted with few direct and specific instructions from politicians on high. Policy bureaucracies produce policies complete with detail—including specification of precise measures needed to give effect to policies, precise legal clauses required to allow them to be put in place, guidance and other forms of protocols about how they should work in practice, and some idea of any future arrangements that have to be put in place to make the policy work or maintain it. The policymaking process does not invariably produce regulations or other measures that cover every last detail of a policy—something which is impossible and often undesirable as many issues may be left for later resolution whether by subsequent regulations or delegation to others (see Thatcher and Stone Sweet 2003; Page 2001). Nevertheless, policies typically involve the specification of a level of detail that requires a familiarity with, among other things, the issue under consideration, the policy machinery, law, and precedent, which politicians cannot generally be expected to have. By their nature political leaders cannot be expected to give close directions or instructions over how to do policy work—even if they had the expertise, they are unlikely to have the time to issue tight instructions about the choices to be made by those developing policies.

The question of how politicians control policy bureaucracies is conventionally answered by a largely implicit notion of a hierarchy of policy decisions, similar to a 'static hierarchy of norms' (Kelsen 1945: 112–13) in Continental legal theory. Broadly this term means that key or strategic political choices, made by politicians or politicians in conjunction with group representatives and senior officials, shape the contours of policy. The policy work that goes on in policy bureaucracies develops the measures that follow from this strategic decision—with policy work of the sort described in Chapters 2 and 3 as embellishment and detail, to use a phrase that more commonly describes a different aspect of political life in Britain—class voting (Pulzer 1967: 98). This hierarchy is closely linked to the commonplace distinction between 'policy' and 'administration'. It leads to the assumption that bureaucrats, and above all those below the top, are involved in 'implementation'. Wilson and Barker (2003: 370) claim that the UK civil service has been moving away from a role in the 1970s and 1980s in which officials were involved in policymaking 'towards the more traditional . . . [model] in which politicians decide on policy and bureaucrats implement it' with 'excessive subordination of bureaucrats to politicians'.

This chapter shows that those who work in policy bureaucracies are not—both by grade and importance in shaping policy—essentially subordinates with the simple task of working out the consequential details of the big strategic decisions taken by senior people who are closer to the political action. That such a view appears predominant in the study of public policy might be explained through its conformity with democratic theory (as it gives the key role in the policy process, even in a bureaucratic political system, to elected officials), through the fact that it makes the study of public policy easier (as it suggests that one has to talk only to the top people to find out how key decisions were arrived at), and through the possibility that it fits Anglo-American cultural norms about what 'decisions' are. As the legal theorist Damaška (1986: 47–8) puts it, the Anglo-American world looks at policy much as it looks at the judicial process: a day in court. In a Common Law understanding of decision-making, once the evidence for and against the defendant is presented, the jury decides and the judgment is passed, all in one arena. This view contrasts with the slower, graduated set of procedures associated with Continental European legal processes. It is the day-in-court versus the long bureaucratic process as caricatured in Kafka's *Der Prozeß* (The Trial), in which the nameless 'man from the country' spends literally his whole lifetime wondering whether he can get past a gatekeeper to reach the law, even though the gatekeeper hardly reassures him by telling him: 'But take note: I am powerful. And I am only the least of the doorkeepers. From hall to hall there is one doorkeeper after another, each more powerful than the last. The third doorkeeper is already so terrible that even I cannot bear to look at him.' The process of policy and policy work is far more elongated and ramshackle than the words 'decision-making' seem to imply, with the idea that there is some discrete act of creation once all the arguments for and against have been amassed. We have to evaluate the influence of middle-ranking officials in this context.

This chapter shows in four ways that processes within policy bureaucracies are not subordinate embellishment and detail. First, the instructions from superiors to which policy officials work are rarely specific enough to guide with any precision the work they do. The notion that politicians delegate is not only well accepted but also a fashionable topic for research; yet what delegation studies tend to look at is the delegation implied in the legislation and other measures that arise from the policy process—whether, for example, bureaucrats in agencies have much discretion in applying regulatory functions given the different regulatory regimes (see Thatcher and Stone Sweet 2002)—rather than forms of delegation in the process of policy formation itself. Second, detail alone does not necessarily characterize the issues policy officials deal with; they are also involved in broader cross-cutting issues. Third, detail is not 'mere detail', since to define details can involve designing the whole shape of the policy. Fourth, significant strategic policy initiatives can be shaped before they ever emerge as such from the work of policy officials. Let us look at each of these in turn.

## The bearable lightness of instruction

In Grimms' fairy tale the daughter of the boastful farmer is locked in a roomful of straw and is expected to use the spinning wheel provided to turn the straw into gold thread before dawn. The raw material on which civil servants doing policy work—especially project work like producing a White Paper, consultation document, piece of legislation, or an internal reform—have to labour is often only marginally more easily convertible to the desired end product. Ministers tend to give some sort of direction that indicates the lines along which they would like their officials to work.

Such communications are usually oral. While, as we will see in Chapter 5, communications upwards tend to be written, communications from the top down are usually oral. A maintenance worker responsible for recommending approval of discretionary financial support for local authorities for a particular set of services described how (rather vague) guidance was given from above to these public bodies to see if they were acting in the spirit of the scheme and thus entitled to the money: 'We got a general steer before Christmas—[there was] a meeting of [the Cabinet subcommittee]. [The results were passed on to us through] the minutes of the meeting [via] my Grade 5 [who] was at the meeting. He saw the ministers and I talked to him.' An official described how the team she worked in was instructed to develop a major piece of legislation:

Number 10 had always had an interest in proceeds of crime, and the PIU decided to look at this (the interest came about, I think, in part because of some specific money laundering problem at the time). This was good for us as the thing now had the weight of Number 10 behind it. The PIU report was published and its 'conclusions' (they don't make 'recommendations' as they are the Cabinet Office) accepted. They sent it all over to us in July 2000 and said 'here you go, now make this work'.

An SEO in the DWP, who was working on the benefits issues arising from an NHS policy document, tells a similar story:

The July 2000 NHS Plan is a DoH document. These are DoH ideas that affect benefits. The NHS Plan will get rid of the preserved rights. Over to you, DWP. The minister says 'OK' and somewhere up there they say 'this is a job for the long-term care team, so do it'.

Many respondents did not have any direct and explicit instructions from anybody to start work on a project. A respondent in charge of reviewing the relationship between her department and a major Non-Departmental Public Body, itself a general priority established in the department's spending review settlement with the Treasury, answered, in response to the question of how she was given the task of looking at the issue:

It was a bit like osmosis. [The permanent secretary] set off the review. We knew it was going along, so we anticipated it coming. So also, as it was a Spending Review year, it became apparent that that is what we are working towards.

Knowing that a policy that falls within your area of responsibility is being discussed is often enough to start work on it.

It was not unknown for ministerial directions to be specific and govern the whole approach an official takes in the project. An official within a department not normally concerned with child-care cited in Chapter 3, who was working on a paper for the minister exploring the possibility of 'informal' childcarers, had already done much of the 'fleshing out' and had raised some problems with it:

[One of our ministers] wanted informal childcare provision. This had been a bee in his bonnet for a few years. The . . . proposals from other departments had not satisfied him. There were too many conditions (you may start as an informal childcarer, but could only receive the allowance if you promised to move to be a registered childminder later on). He wanted [this] department to take it on, to go it alone, but I don't think we can.

Yet among the officials we interviewed, such precision, even as can be found in a minister being dissatisfied with the detailed proposals suggested by others, was rare. At the other extreme the policy directions from politicians could be so broad as to be almost non-existent. An official charged with helping restructure the system of grants to local government (and we interviewed several working on this topic who gave a similar view) suggested that 'ministers do not give a detailed steer on things at the beginning of the process'. Officials knew that the new system they were to come up with should be 'simpler and fairer', yet these goals were rather vague and conflicting since simpler formulae may not necessarily be fairer. One pointed to somewhat clearer objectives for one part of the formula:

> The key brief on the fire formula came right from the top (from the DPM level if not above) to remove a well-known perverse incentive in the formula. The old formula was based on the number of fire calls—the number of times people ring in. But we want fire authorities to reduce the number of calls, false alarms, etc.

Yet saying what the new formula should not include left open the question of what it should. An official who was involved in designing new rules to end the prohibition on taking of blood from unconscious road accident victims to test for alcohol levels gave a shortened version of how the policy was developed.

> It came up because of campaigns. This had been known to be an issue. But what drove the thing was two MPs who had constituents with sons or daughters who had been killed (one was a Government MP and the other from the Opposition). They came to the Home Office, to Charles Clarke, saying something should be done. He got us to look into it and we had discussions with the BMA [British Medical Association], but there were some ethical problems. After discussion with the BMA we had found a way forward to do it. The original idea was to have a Safety Bill from the Department of Transport, Local Government, and the Regions. But we checked with our lawyers who said that the measures were within scope of the Crime and Disorder Bill. We have the way forward so we go to the legal adviser who says 'can be done' and we look at ways of getting it in. The minister would go to the Cabinet Committee to get approval then give the instruction.

The procedure of a general suggestion by the minister that an issue being worked up into a policy be looked into by the officials concerned is, as we will see in later sections, far from unusual.

Officials working on legislation certainly tended to highlight the contrast between what they are expected to produce—highly specific instructions to lawyers that can be converted into as precise a language of law as can be achieved—and the relative vagueness of the material from which they work. Often they work from broad ideas endorsed, possibly even tacitly, by the minister. One HEO(D) working on a long and complex piece of legislation stated:

The principles of what the legislation was meant to do were set out in the White Paper, but only at a very high level of generality. On administration procedures it said they should be 'fairer, quicker, better' but these were high-level ideas. We needed to work out the technical detail.

White Papers and similar documents, such as reports by the Government's own think tank, the PIU, were generally not viewed as offering strong guidance on policy development: 'The White Paper was open' was a sentiment expressed by most officials who had to write legislation. A lawyer who dealt with policy officials working on a major piece of legislation commented:

We need to give detail. They [the specialist legislative drafters] need an idea of how to approach the issue. So we have to go into great detail— really, really detailed. In my period with the Proceeds of Crime Bill all I did was attend meetings and write instructions...we were trying to create something new and difficult....The intention [behind the bill] is the basis for instructions and we have to take it to such levels of detail that nobody who thought of the original intention would have thought of [the level of detail and issues we cover]. Our job and that of [the specialist legislative drafters] is intellectually stretching. Some of the things we get into are difficult. Really tough things and you get a real satisfaction from getting them right. If the policy is not clear then it won't work.

While we will look at the cues officials use to develop policies in Chapter 5, the central point is that for project development, many crucial dimensions of what a policy should look like are vague at the time a policy official first starts work on it.

Lack of direct ministerial instruction also characterizes service and maintenance work, but is far less apparent in these activities since officials' job descriptions—such as working in a private office or responsibility for making sure that a cross-departmental sustainability initiative is taken seriously by other departments—make their work less directly responsive to an individual initiative. Even here ministers tend not to be explicit about what they want and it is up to civil servants to find out. A fast streamer working in the private office of a Secretary of State, when asked how he knew whether his minister needed to see any particular document or whether it could be handled without passing it on to the minister, responded:

Your judgement develops over time. You observe how her interests develop and what she is interested in. Is it a key issue that could derail policy or is it not? It is a judgement that develops. Two of the private secretaries [HEOs] are new. I can see them getting to grips with this now just like I did. You have to shield her against being overwhelmed and prioritize things for her.

While ministerial influence does not, as we shall see, finish after the initial green light is given to develop policy—there are plenty of opportunities for ministers to shape the policy right up until it becomes operative and even after that—the fact that ministerial directions at this early stage, where given, tend to be rather general leaves substantial room for officials to have significant influence in the early stages of policy development, above all, but not limited to, deciding the scope of a policy (what should be included and excluded from it) and developing its initial contours.

## Taking the broader view

The notion that broader strategic policy decisions shape the subsequent policy work suggests that the big political issues have already been resolved and that policy work is simply a matter of working through the embellishment and detail. In favour of this argument one might cite the Whitehall studies of Sir Michael Marmot and colleagues that find a correlation between 'decision latitude' perceived by civil servants in their everyday work and grade—the more senior, the greater decision latitude and control over one's pace of work (see Kuper and Marmot 2003). To put this finding in perspective, however, the correlation is strong but not overwhelming (+ 0.51); the grades we are looking at are the second, third, and fourth out of six used in the Whitehall studies (the SCS is Marmot's top grade) in terms of grade groupings, and thus Grade 7s are among those with most 'decision latitude'; and, perhaps most importantly, the Whitehall studies do not look at officials doing policy work only.

While detail is an important part of policy work, there are two problems with the assumption that the big strategic decisions are taken at the top and that the lower grades do the monotonous detail. The first is that detail is not the only issue policy officials deal with—their work takes them into broader political areas that make any original 'strategic' policy decision by a politician seem narrow by comparison. The second is that detail cannot be separated from strategy, since to work out details one has to define or redefine what might be termed strategic objectives. This second problem is dealt with in the next section. Here the concern is with the broader issues policy officials have to deal with.

*Joining things up*

While it is often assumed that coordination is a matter for the higher levels of the bureaucracy, relatively junior officials have significant responsibility for policy coordination. As we will see in the next chapter, invoking the support or the authority of a minister is important if agreement cannot be reached, but much 'joining up' of government takes place at this level without ministerial involvement. As an HEO responsible for developing the Stonehenge site, in which English Heritage, the Highways Agency, and the National Trust were also involved, put it:

What I have done is establish what was going on. Then I elbowed my way to meetings. We were giving money but not having any direct involvement. This meant taking a more active coordination role and bashing heads together quite politely. The job was to get people to realize that the two projects [involved in the Stonehenge development] were interdependent and to get some handle on budgetary control.

Even where ministers are called in to be involved in interdepartmental issues, their participation may be a formality, as one Grade 7 suggested:

We had difficulties with [the other department] and [the minister] wrote [to them] about the sticky bits. In fact, I'd agreed the best way forward with the other department, but they said they'd want it put in a letter from our minister to theirs. We agreed the draft letter with the other department, the minister wrote it, and the people I'd been talking to drafted the reply. In fact they could not imagine the minister would have a difficulty with what was in the letter we sent, so they could start drafting the response before the letter was sent.

Even fairly sensitive interdepartmental issues can be dealt with without direct intervention of ministers:

The last thing I did on this was drafting a protocol with the Prison Service. [*Interviewer: Was it published on the web?*] Well . . . [pause] it was an internal administrative thing. . . . Well it was a turf thing, agreeing with the prison service the proper lines of demarcation and responsibilities.

The notion that such cross-cutting issues are to be resolved by passing things upwards is inaccurate; 'joining things up' is a major part of the work of policy bureaucrats in the grades we examined.

The policy work of some departments is heavily geared towards interdepartmental activity. The Social Exclusion Unit (SEU), set up under New Labour to develop cross-cutting policy initiatives, effectively shapes policy by working with other departments. For a Grade 7 in the SEU 'joining up' government was a major part of her work:

The project I am working on . . . [means trying] to join up policy in government departments. The key point is to take a specific problem and look at what the Government can do. The education of children in care project came about as children in care do especially badly in education. As a team we have been analysing the problems—why children in care are let down—and coming up with recommendations. The evidence side means going out and talking to people. . . . We met key stakeholders and worked with other departments, notably the DoH and the DfES. We got a good idea of why children in care are not able to reach their potential. The obvious reason is that they are not in school, and why not? Because social workers simply don't have time to get them into schools.

Moreover, much of the policy work in the Treasury is geared towards interdepartmental activities. Treasury officials have an especially strong hand in interdepartmental negotiations because of the Treasury's political power, status, and financial control. A Treasury Grade 7 said:

Yes, [rooms do fall quiet when you come into the room as a Treasury man] the Treasury has that sort of reputation. This can be helpful when you're negotiating with other departments. It can be tiresome, especially as I'm not from a Treasury background and not attracted by the Treasury way of saying 'no' in 101 creative ways. I've been in Brussels and know that compromise is useful and that an intransigent Treasury can be a pain in the arse.

The status of the department strengthens the hand of interdepartmentally focused positions. Several respondents from inside and outside the SEU commented on its loss of status on its transfer from the Cabinet Office, and of the close association with the Prime Minister's own policy agenda, to the ODPM. One sympathetic outside observer of the Unit commented: 'Yes, they had more sway as part of the Cabinet Office than they have now. Now they are a bit more . . . [hesitates] . . . they have not quite found their feet, not knowing what being in the ODPM means. They can, of course, use the DPM and he can help them.' Yet in this case probably proximity to the Prime Minister rather than the Cabinet Office itself conferred the status. Another official associated with illegal drugs policy suggested that the movement out of the Cabinet Office to the Home Office meant that 'the drugs units have more powerful ministers in the Home Office than the Cabinet Office'.

We also came across two officials who could be classed as 'troubleshooters' from the Cabinet Office who had moved to parts of departments that needed some external help. One, a former Cabinet Office official, responded to the question of whether he was sent in by the Cabinet Office to 'sort out' his new department:

The full answer to me being here is that [the permanent secretary in this department] among other senior management is the person trying to push the [Department's] change strategy through—the idea is to make it the sort of place you would want to work in, you can come in here, get things done, and make your mark. That meant moving people in to do the work. If you are trying to deliver significant change, the thinking was you don't want people steeped in [the department's] history.

Another official was transferred from the Cabinet Office's PIU into the DoH (although she had previously worked in the DoH but in a different part of the ministry) to help ensure the 'modernization' agenda was reflected in work on proposed new legislation in which the PIU had had a hand. But we did not find any other cases of officials being sent out to work in departments to fulfil a 'coordinating' or even 'troubleshooting' mission for key institutions such as the Treasury or the Cabinet Office.

### Getting the UK angle

Policy officials frequently deal with the relationship between the policy for which they are responsible and the non-English parts of the UK. Among the issues dealt with by our respondents, such issues were rarely settled before policy work began on them, and settling them was an important part of the policy work. The modes of dealing with the non-English parts of the UK varied substantially. In reserved matters where the devolved administrations had no responsibility, this merely meant informing their counterparts in Cardiff, Belfast, or Edinburgh what they were proposing to do. An official responsible for developing UK-wide legislation described his role:

[T]here wasn't much Scottish negotiation. It was a matter of keeping them informed and getting their views. My recollection is that we got a few letters saying 'bear in mind x, y, and z' and nothing more. These were reserved powers. The thing to do is to inform them. They'll jump up and down if you don't send a letter in time, but there is not much input from them—they know where the line is drawn [with reserved powers].

One official helping develop legislation implementing EU law described how there was little negotiation with the devolved administrations although she was covering issues that came under their powers:

My team also effectively wrote most of the Scottish, Welsh, and Northern Irish regs [regulations] too . . . they don't have the resources to do it and it would be a wasted duplication of effort. They have to see it and understand it of course to make sure they agree and that we are not pulling a fast one, but we were very much in the lead. Eventually they made their own regs based on our regs. There was a lot of work involved in this as we are trying to keep all four bits of the UK in harness here, to make sure we have mutual trust and that we transposed in a pretty much uniform way. [*Interviewer: When you were doing the Welsh and Scottish regs did you go to Edinburgh and Cardiff?*] No, they come here, but it's mostly done by email.

Yet for others, handling the Scottish, Welsh, and Northern Ireland dimensions often involved exploring a territorial approach to policy development not settled in any original policy announcement.

One of our respondents was involved in an intensely political conflict concerning Whitehall, senior members of a devolved government, the Treasury, and Number 10 over the Barnett Formula, which allocates spending to different parts of the UK. The incident concerned perceptions by the devolved administration that 'the Barnett Formula did not give them enough'. The devolved ministers insisted on a meeting with the Chancellor, and our respondent had to brief him. The devolved administration made claims about the dire consequences of them not getting the extra money and even sought to enlist the support of the Prime

Minister. The job of the Treasury, and the respondent, was 'not to let them get away with it'.

In developing one piece of legislation, the Proceeds of Crime Act 2002, there was extensive collaboration between the Home Office officials in charge of drafting it and officials from the Scottish Executive. At the Scottish Labour Conference in March 2003, the Secretary of State for Scotland, Helen Liddell, described the Act as 'the biggest piece of Scottish legislation passed at Westminster since devolution'.[21] Although it was the subject of a Sewel Motion,[22] a parliamentary device to allow legislation passed in Westminster to apply to Scotland even in devolved areas (in fact it was the first use of a Sewel Motion), the issue was largely handled by policy officials within middle grades. Some issues were firmly established political priorities in handling the Scottish end. Two related questions were the territorial jurisdiction of an Assets Recovery Agency (ARA) and the use in Scotland of civil procedures to seize money and goods gained by criminal activity. As a Scottish official involved put it:

The starting point was that the Lord Advocate was determined to hold on to his confiscation powers, [and properly so]. . . . [I]t was an option to argue that the ARA should have powers in Scotland. Ministers agreed that the Lord Advocate should retain his confiscation powers. But then we had to look at civil recovery and taxation. One option was to set up a separate agency. That was ruled out because of the small number of civil recoveries we were thinking of. And a quango would be top heavy and bureaucratic. And at that time the then First Minister Henry McLeish was on one of the periodic tacks taken here in Scotland about bonfires of quangos. . . . [T]he idea of an English quango extending to Scotland was not politically acceptable. As far as civil recovery goes, it was decided to do this in the name of the Scottish ministers.

On many other issues the room for negotiation was large. As one of the English participants observed of the Scottish part of the process:

Our lawyers checked to make sure that the [English and Scottish] schemes were compatible. [*Interviewer: Were there any problems?*] Yes, but nothing insurmountable. . . . This did not involve discussions at ministerial level—we sorted things out at the official level. . . . It was just a matter of reaching a compromise. A lot of times they'd decide to do things the way we wanted to do it, other times we did it their way. The idea is to make the provisions as similar as possible between England and Wales and Scotland.

Another pointed out: 'In each case where we identified a policy difference, we'd look at why it was there and what path we needed to follow.' In interview, when presented with this rather idyllic account of how Whitehall officials willingly gave ground on one particular disagreement after they had listened to the reasoned arguments of their Scottish brethren, a Scottish Executive official reacted: 'Did they hell! On this one there were two of us [policy officials from the Scottish Executive] and a few solicitors against the whole army of civil servants and solicitors from Whitehall. We held out.' The relations between the Home Office officials and the Scottish Executive officials who moved to London for much of the preparation of the Bill were warm, friendly even. But there were significant clashes between them that were resolved often at the (middle-ranking) official level, sometimes with the Scottish officials threatening to 'wheel the ministers in' as one put it, to support their case, and occasionally doing so.

While consultation seeking Scottish views is common, especially among officials representing Whitehall departments in the EU, the flow of consultation can also go the other way—Scottish officials asking for an English view of Scottish legislation. As one Whitehall official commented:

At this precise moment I am offering comments on a draft guidance being issued by the Scottish Executive on free personal care. This has a direct impact on people in our homes. . . . Social care and social security provisions are related, but social care is devolved and social security Great Britain-wide. . . . The Scottish Executive decided to go its own way. There was a row between the [Whitehall] ministers and the devolved ministers on the issue. It was resolved last autumn, and this is the final knockings of it. I was heavily involved with the ministers on this. There was a grate [or friction] between social security policy and social care. There is often a working through to the social security system. Housing Benefit colleagues get a lot of this on a regular basis, this is relatively new to us. It looks OK now [points to draft guidance that is on his computer screen]. I'm just cross-checking that everything is as it should be.

One Whitehall official saw her Scottishness as an advantage in dealing with her fellows on devolved matters: 'We usually see eye to eye. Because of my [Scottish] accent they don't perceive me as a Westminster type with a posh accent trying to lick them into shape.'

Much of the broader issue of fitting policy into a UK context is handled at the middle level of policy bureaucracies. There are limits to what can be settled at this level that are explored in Chapter 5. Moreover, threatening to 'wheel in' a minister can offer the possibility of settling political issues without directly involving politicians. But the idea that policy bureaucracy is simply about subordinate issues ignores the important role officials have in the broader issues of intra-UK political and administrative relations.

## Human rights

Human rights issues cannot be construed as a simple technical matter of implementation. Since the passage of the 1998 Human Rights Act, UK policy initiatives must conform to the European Declaration of Human Rights guaranteeing a variety of personal freedoms. The task of devising policies consistent with the Act and unlikely successfully to be challenged in the courts is hardly a matter of detail; yet it is one of the functions of the policy officials we spoke to rather than an issue settled at the top. A solicitor dealing with members of a team developing legislation outlined part of her role in developing the legislation:

You have a policy that sounds OK when you do the policy papers. Our job is to look at it and see that there are not any legal issues—do you need new legislation? What do you want—do you want it clear in the bill or in the regulations what you want to do? Are there wider issues—a duty to consult the European Convention on Human Rights [ECHR]? We have to draft an ECHR memorandum—before the Bill has its second reading the minister has to sign a certificate saying it is consistent with the ECHR. The ECHR memorandum [where the compatibility of the legislation with ECHR is set out] is a pretty tortuous process.

A policy official on a different bill team dealing with the issue of the seizure of criminal assets argued:

The biggest difficulty was to devise a scheme that was compliant with the Human Rights Act [*Interviewer: Was this something that there was external pressure on you to do?*] No, we're all aware of the Human Rights Act. Of course the legal adviser did say what was wrong with things as we went along, but we also knew about it. For example, the Irish scheme [we were interested in learning from] has at some stage in the proceedings a reverse burden of proof. We knew we would not pursue this aspect of the scheme because of the Human Rights Act. I think there is a history of correspondence between us and the [legal] advisers on this—there is quite an established lengthy correspondence with the lawyers on the compatibility of the Irish and other schemes with the HRA.

Human rights issues can have fundamental impact on the character of policy measures, frequently cutting across a range of core measures in any legislation. Dealing with such issues is often an important part of the policy work of middle-ranking officials, especially those working in production jobs.

## Europe

Interacting with the EU was an important function of many of our middle-ranking officials. Maintenance work often involves liaising with the institutions of the EU and representing a department in negotiations and discussions in Brussels. For example, one Grade 7 official in DEFRA is responsible for advising on the agriculture parts of the EU budget:

It is not a financial accounting role but a policy role. . . . The EU spends €45 billion on agriculture and I provide the UK line on that. . . . I provide it via the Council, via the committee responsible for that programme in the budget in Brussels, and via a working group that looks at proposals for reform. . . . I am over in Brussels around twice a month. This week we are heading into CAP [Common Agricultural Policy] negotiations at Council level. I am responsible for letting the minister know [how the money is being spent].

She went on to describe how she worked on the budget to come up with a UK line:

[I]f there are any changes in [the budget] . . . we are concerned. If we get any changes proposed I will go to the people who know the agricultural product concerned. I will, say, go to the cereals production people, then I will put together a draft UK line, I will check it with the Treasury and check elsewhere in DEFRA. . . . If there is a change in legislation we have a departmental committee on Europe that meets every week. My director, a Grade 3, chairs the meeting, and it is where we discuss forthcoming policy proposals and go through the UK line on policy proposals. I go along to these meetings most of the time—there is usually something on money there. I have to say something about the policy and how much we will need to spend on it, and I go to the economists to see if there are value-for-money issues we need to look at.

This is not a matter of a single official 'deciding' a UK policy line—there is no single point of decision on most issues and the involvement of ministers and top officials in this will be explored further in Chapter 5—but officials at this level play a crucial role in establishing the UK line.

The European linkage was especially important for DEFRA respondents, and the intricacies of establishing a UK line could be complex. A significant focus on EU activity was found in respondents from four other departments too. A Treasury official involved in DEFRA policies pointed out his role in helping shape the UK line in EU negotiations:

I tend not to spend all that much time in Brussels—mainly for the time it takes up. The main sources of information we have about what is going on out there are DEFRA and the Foreign Office (above all UKREP [UK Permanent Representation to the EU]). . . . A lot of time is spent formulating the UK government's position on an issue. For example, the EU-wide emissions trading permits. We spend a lot of time on evaluating the

Commission proposal and determining what changes we would like—seeing how we should amend article x or y.

An MoD official described his work on European defence:

My section deals with European Security and Defence Policy—[ESDP]. It is headed by the Principal ... and three desk officials—two civilian and one military. Collectively what we do is develop and seek to implement UK policy on ESDP. This involves original thinking—what should we all be doing in five or ten years' time and what do we do to bring this about.... But the blue skies thinking gets submerged under the things that come in by way of initiatives from outside—from our partners, the EU and the Commission and so on. We have to decide how what they are proposing fits in with our aspirations in the field of ESDP. The Principal tends to lead and deal with the overarching issues. The three desk officers have responsibilities for particular bits of ESDP.... I don't tend to be given things that are long-term, such as EU–NATO relations. As a result I do some of the peripheral things, such as Galileo (Europe's answer to the Strategic Defence Initiative). Having said this I'm now going to contradict myself by saying that I am starting to work on the Convention on the Future of Europe—Giscard d'Estaing's.... Though they are talking about getting something in quick.

A fast streamer in the DTI described her role in European affairs:

My task at the moment is that the EU decided to create an entrepreneurship Green Paper, and my job is to get in there at an early stage and shape the Green Paper, not just the UK bits of it but the whole Green Paper. So I have done twenty-five pages on how the Green Paper should look: setting the scene, what entrepreneurship needs, and an annex with best practice from the UK, and the idea is that other countries put in best practice from there too. The idea is to shape the Green Paper by getting some ideas in there first.

We also came across officials within the DWP developing the UK position on proposed EU measures on immigrant workers.

## Elaborating policy and detail

The idea that a middle-ranking official is likely to deal with relatively narrow matters in part arises from the semantic ease with which 'detail' can be associated with 'narrow'. Developing policy requires familiarity with detail, but this detail can be very closely tied up with the question of how one deals with much broader cross-cutting issues as elaborated in the last section. Furthermore, it is not always easy to separate broad strategy from detail. Middle-ranking officials in policy bureaucracies do many things that qualify, at least for the outside observer, as 'uninteresting detail'. Running a contract that involves evaluating a programme already in action would be an example of policy work that has, at least on face value, less to do with shaping policy and more with preparing evidence on the basis of which broader strategic decisions may be taken. However, when developing policy, it is common for the policy and the detail to be considered at the same time. Policies are often presented to officials to work on in rather vague terms. How officials elaborate policies therefore often involves making it less vague—by specifying how it might work.

We came across numerous examples of officials shaping broader principles of policy through elaboration of how a policy might work in practice. The bill team members who drafted primary legislation offered perhaps the clearest example. One lawyer advising the team on the Proceeds of Crime Bill pointed out:

The difficult thing about this Bill was that nobody knew the details of all of it. Originally there were two of us on it and we did not know all of it, but I was the only one who knew all of it once I was on my own. . . . What I had to do in August 2001 was to stand back and look at the whole thing and define how we would deal with the cross-cutting issues—this was before the introduction. This hinges around the Director of the Assets Recovery Agency. [This is not one of those bills that is made up of a variety of different bits]. There is one concept running through it—the proceeds of criminal conduct. It comes up in all different places and I had to make sure that the same thing runs all the way through in these different places where it comes up so that people cannot pick holes in it.

One official in one of the bill teams pointed out that an apparently small matter could have huge implications outside the particular area concerned:

One policy issue that came up, and this is a normal big bill point, was whether the legislation gave [the government body concerned sufficient powers]. It looked like a detailed point but turned out to get thornier and thornier.... One of the biggest problems was that we realized that we had something that affected, if our worries were right, how an awful lot of legislation was phrased. Although [one] lawyer said there was a problem, we had huge trouble persuading Parliamentary Counsel that we had a problem. He was worried about the shadow our bill could cast over a whole load of statutory provisions—if we changed it how we wanted it, it would show up problems in other legislation. You sometimes get a detail which takes you into major policy and to thinking about what you can do about it. A problem you often get in a bill—a minor tweak becomes a huge issue. It has happened on all legislation I've been on.

All officials interviewed who were developing legislation pointed to the interrelationship between their drafting work and the development of what might be termed 'strategic' policy issues (see Page 2003 for more discussion of this aspect).

This aspect of middle-ranking civil servants' work—involvement in 'strategic' issues through the development of apparent 'detail'—was a common theme of other interviews. An SEO, who was asked to look at ways of increasing the number of childcarers through 'informal' carers, declared:

There are all sorts of complexities—this is at a very early stage. We are going to ministers to see if they want us to do more work. There are lots of knock on effects—what is the employment status of these informal carers, do they get paid at national minimum wage, how does it fit in with JobCentre Plus, the new tax credits, what if the carers are pensioners?

The complexities of the question may well make this issue difficult to take forward. A Grade 7 in the DoH was working on some guidelines for the sensitive question of financial support for the elderly in care homes. Even though they were 'guidelines', they had important financial implications and provoked substantial controversy:

The consultation over the practice guidelines was just as hard—harder even [than developing guidance on the law to which they relate]. In the statutory guidance you can skate over the details, but you have to develop them in the practice guidance. There are two areas where there is some debate. Advice about benefits—how to set up benefits advice centres. Another is in assessing the costs of disability. The theory is that one person who is a specialist can ask what the disability is and what needs to be spent on it. This leads to a means test. Assessment of disability expenditure is a very fraught area. People say, for example, the disability involves extra clothing or laundry costs. This raises the question of what is 'extra'—what is 'normal' come to think of it? That is all part of the consultation.

Even the most strategic of issues, the long-term forward-planning process of a major department, could be shaped by a middle-ranking official. An SEO, concerned with putting together the detailed guidelines about how to plan, said:

Last year there was a discussion at management board level about what was wanted in the [departmental] plan. The [last] plan was top heavy with detail—lots of objectives and lots of targets. People felt that if their [part of the budget] was not in the plan they would not be represented, so everyone wanted their [part of the budget] in it. After a year I and my immediate boss [at Grade 7] decided it was too unwieldy.... We set the agenda. I said '[this time] let's have three objectives' [and this part of the process] was developed at my level.

Even the activity of running an established programme can bring officials into making choices with implications for the strategic future of the policy. Local Public Service Agreements (PSAs) are quasi-contracts between government departments and local government authorities managed by the ODPM. The local government authorities volunteer to set and deliver on 'challenging' performance targets and in return receive money from HM Treasury. Whether these targets work depends crucially on whether the individual schemes have challenging targets and whether local authorities are judged to have met them, and developing these targets is the work of a team of middle-ranking officials. A Grade 7 involved described her work:

[What do we do if the targets are not in the spirit of the scheme?] We go back and ask questions. Because we are providing a reward grant, we have to have a sort of general view that what is being offered is worth it. This can be big money. For example, [a northern county council] gets £2 million for each target if it reaches them, so we have to justify the amount if asked. Sometimes this is just asking 'what does this mean?' and 'what period are you counting?' Quite often they will change it. They have to persuade us that it is worthwhile. . . . This has to be signed off by ministers and we put them before ministers. They are interdepartmental so they go to other ministers. It is possible for one minister to be outvoted, but there have been no cases of disagreement yet. In theory it can happen. [*Interviewer: How do you work out if the council has offered a valid target?*] It is hard as the targets are in all sorts of areas. In some cases we have to accept that the other department knows best. One set of things we challenge them on is that they produce real outcomes. There is an issue that they must be looking at outcomes rather than process. . . . The aim is to get an agreement without ministers. I don't think we have had anything with a disagreement between ministers. Perhaps we should have done, but we have not.

A Grade 7 official involved in a major social policy initiative argued:

The team leader [and his or her colleagues] is the bunch that does a lot of the donkey work and gets a lot of the stick. At the moment it is boiling in my area. The way the policy is being developed, and the operational experience coming back to us, is demonstrating that the policy has problems. So people like me step in not only to say 'I told you so' but also to put things right.

He went on to describe what he meant by talking about a set of decisions he was currently involved in. Ostensibly the decision was about a minor matter of timing—allowing a little longer than envisaged for the transition from one regime to another. But he suggested more was at stake than timing:

One argument against giving them more time is that the whole point behind [this initiative] was that it should be a culture change—redefining the way that services were packaged and . . . [delivered]. If we are not careful that won't happen. The longer it goes on and the longer you give for adjustment, you tend to come back to the status quo. Then you have to ask: 'what is the point of it all'? You upset the apple cart for two to three years and then have to ask whether we really brought about change. And the people who were reformed to make way for the new regime will come back and say that the only 'new' thing in this is what we were doing anyway.

The cliché about the devil being in the detail is nevertheless a generally accepted premise that points out, even if it does not much illuminate, a common feature of policy work.

## The initiation of policy

Policy officials can be involved in initiating policy. Initiating policies often arises from maintenance or support work—observing or keeping an eye on an issue helps generate ideas for new policy initiatives. Some policy initiation can cover issues that arouse relatively little controversy. A Grade 7 in the DfES outlined a useful initiative she had a large part in getting off the ground about how to transfer pupil records from one local education authority to another. The initiative meant devising a system that schools would be able to use, getting data services in the DfES to design the interface and the programme, developing safeguards to comply with the Data Protection Act, piloting and publicizing the initiative.

This was very stimulating and very rewarding. For once you are doing something that people want and had a clear benefit. It was very demanding but I was really proud of it. We pushed ourselves on this. It was all done in six weeks. We started in August and it was delivered on 18 September.

Another Grade 7 official from the same department pointed out how he developed a new strand to the 'welfare to work' policies of the New Labour Government aimed at making it easier for people with disabilities to remain in employment.

How did it come about? Partly from observing what was going on. We were piloting something else, and the pilot was not being very effective. It was my responsibility and I took a close interest in how it was going. I realized that there was an issue with people in danger of losing their jobs because of disability or ill health before the evaluative data came out. I was running the pilot. I held the contracts with the providers—I actually went out to the pilots. I went out to the social security offices and began to realize that something was not going well. The twin aim of the pilots was to bring people from welfare into work and to stop people in work losing their jobs, and this second aim was not being fulfilled. How to identify people at risk of losing their job requires an extra set-up—it could not be done within the existing set-up. I then began thinking about an alternative approach.

This then became part of the larger 'Job Retention' pilot scheme, which included innovative experiments aimed at increasing employment prospects, each of which is subject to rigorous evaluation of its effects (see Morris et al. 2003).

While it would be mistaken to argue that significant numbers of our respondents initiated the kinds of policies that find their way into party election manifestos, two of the four bill teams we studied (discussed in Appendix A, see Page 2003 for a fuller discussion) started life with the significant involvement of middle-ranking officials and then were taken up by the Labour Party in its 2001 election manifesto (see Labour Party 2001). The Proceeds of Crime Bill 2002 started life as the Third Report of the 1998 Working Group on Confiscation (Home Office 1998). Three members of this team were members of the later bill team, including the head of the bill team and chair of the Working Group, who was a Grade 5, and two Grade 7s. While the policy development also went through the policy unit within the Cabinet Office with close links to the Prime Minister, the PIU (which later became the Prime Minister's Strategy Unit), the policy development rested primarily with the Home Office officials—with the PIU having a greater impact on the political visibility of the issue, marking it out as a prime ministerial priority. Moreover two Home Office officials who had served on the Working Group and later on the bill team were also members of the team that produced the PIU Report. The Land Registration Act 2002 was different in the sense that it started life primarily because of the skill, intellect, and activism of one Law Commissioner, Charles Harpum[23]—a senior barrister on loan from the Office of Parliamentary Counsel—and not a group of officials operating around the middle grades of the civil service. Yet the Act was a collaboration between the Law Commission and the Land Registry, and two members of the bill team were involved in the early days of the Law Commission/ Land Registry working party that produced the legislation (Law Commission 1998; 2001) and two other advisers were also involved with the early generation of the legislation. This legislative proposal was adopted in the Labour 2001 manifesto: common reasons given for its adoption were that it linked with the New Labour 'modernizing' agenda (it brought land registration into the digital age), and the technically high quality of the proposed legislation was attractive to the Lord Chancellor, Lord Irvine of Lairg.

Policy initiation on a major as well as a minor scale, or at least significant involvement in initiation, can arise from the everyday activities of middle-ranking officials. As a Grade 7 in the MoD responsible for relations with NATO described it, the initiative could be rather unexpected:

A large part of the work is briefing. Occasionally we take it on ourselves to write a paper. I have just done a paper suggesting ways forward for integrating new members in the Alliance; 80 per cent of the time these things don't come to anything. Occasionally you do a paper that gets shown around to other allies, and it could get backing and put into NATO and can be policy. I am occasionally doing bits like that (I've done two or three in the last year). That is 10 per cent of the time, 50 per cent is briefing and the rest is all sorts of small things.

Briefings by middle-ranking officials can themselves end up as ministers' own ideas, which they also take up in more elevated policy forums. A Grade 7 argued that he had a significant role in initiating some of the aspects of the cross-departmental initiative for which he was responsible:

We . . . [hesitates and chooses his words carefully] I cannot say that we drafted the [report on which the policy was based], the [body responsible for the report] is an independent agency, but let us say we were aware of what their recommendations would be and we were happy with them.

They went to [the relevant] Cabinet Committee. [Our junior minister sits on it and it is chaired by our Secretary of State]. [Our junior minister] went along to the Committee with the recommendations we wrote for him. It was about how to improve things in the [next spending review]. And another thing was about getting data on [how existing policy is being delivered]. Those were the big ones [issues] to go forward.

We certainly do not want to create the impression that policy initiation is a major function of policy work—it is not. By selecting respondents from bill teams we were likely to find this kind of activity overrepresented among our respondents. Nevertheless, even outside bill teams it is possible to find examples of middle-ranking policy bureaucrats involved in significant cases of policy initiation, contrary to the expectations of much of the academic literature (see Kingdon 1985).

## Conclusions

Middle-ranking officials are involved in the creative process of policy making, however one chooses to define this term. None of the characteristics of what are often deemed to be the truly important parts of the process—dealing with the 'broader picture', shaping the 'broad contours' of policy, or even 'initiating' it—rules them out. Not only are they in contact with the people who matter in making decisions, or are even in the same room when decisions are made, but they also participate actively in shaping policy decisions.

This conclusion must be immediately qualified by emphasizing that we are not claiming that middle-ranking civil servants shape policy according to their own, or even a 'civil service', set of values. Our respondents never gave the impression that they felt they influenced things by seeing their own preferences or desires reflected in the final policy. They showed they were closely and actively involved in developing policy, bringing them into close contact with senior politicians and top-level policymaking institutions such as Cabinet Committees and Number 10 think tanks. Indeed, as far as we can tell from the interviews we conducted, this close involvement with high-level policymaking seems to be a main attraction of policy work. But at the same time, while they had discretion, not least because ministerial directions were often very loose, they never felt they had much discretion to shape things the way they personally wanted to. How they exercised the discretion they had without necessarily introducing their own preferences and agendas into the policy process is explained in Chapter 5.

# 5

# Discretion, Cues and Authority

## Discretion and responsibility

Policy bureaucrats in the middle grades are decision-makers. It is difficult to think of anyone, and certainly anyone in government, who is not a decision-maker of sorts, whether politician, civil servant, front-line administrator or service provider (Lipsky 1980). The term is so broad as to be virtually meaningless. As far as the term refers to people who make *political* decisions, the content of the issues they help decide does not distinguish middle-ranking policy bureaucrats from politicians, as they deal with the same issues as occupy politicians (Chapter 4). The difference between the role of bureaucrats, even middle-level bureaucrats, and politicians is less the content of what they are involved in than in levels of responsibility involved in making any choices. Weber (1988: 837) argued that the essential difference between an official and a politician was that the politician has 'responsibility for things he has made his own'. Ultimately this principle meant that political roles entailed securing desired objectives through attracting and mobilizing political support. Political activity differs from bureaucratic activity, which is essentially subordinate. A bureaucrat at whatever level is in the service of others. While, according to Weber, the politician can say 'either this happens or I resign', the bureaucrat cannot. The official is both duty- and honour-bound to carry out the politician's wishes, even if he disagrees with them, 'as if they resulted from his own most personally held convictions'.

Making policy decisions as a subordinate within an organization is a highly constrained activity. Scholars have recently tended to assume that administrators have discretion when there are no rules to guide their actions—discretion begins where regulation ends. Huber and Shipan (2002) argue that administrative discretion is constrained by the volume of discrete instructions contained in any formal regulations. The more the law has to say, the less the administrators' room for manoeuvre. Moreover, it is common to assume that in exercising this discretion, bureaucrats follow personal preferences. Such preferences may be based on family background and socialization experiences, as suggested by the literature on 'representative bureaucracy' (see Sheriff 1976; Sowa and Selden 2003), or on rational self-interest, usually meaning some material benefit (see Niskanen 1971) or on some perception of desired organizational or programmatic objectives (Downs 1967; Dunleavy 1991).

When applied to policy bureaucracies, both assumptions—that discretion fills the gaps left by regulation and that personal motives or perceptions drive its exercise—offer a highly misleading account of bureaucratic behaviour in general and bureaucratic roles in policymaking in particular. This chapter starts by showing that policy bureaucracies certainly do not appear to be organizations that observe the formalities of hierarchy, and that while senior officials have important roles in supervising the work of middle-ranking policy officials, giving direct instructions, and even scrutinizing what their subordinates in the middle grades do, they are not particularly prominent among them. If bureaucrats are not guided by instructions from superiors, what cues do they use to make their decisions? The short answer is they use a variety of cues that boil down to the same thing: indicators of what is likely to be acceptable to ministers.

All public policy change has to be developed on the basis of explicit ministerial approval—not only change affecting high policy but also that which appears to come closer to repetitive routine. Anything that a ministry commits itself to has to be approved by a minister, whether the commitment is contained in a new circular or code of guidance, a bargaining stance for departmental representatives in diverse EU and other international forums, the ouline of a direction to be pursued in a White Paper or consultation document, an agreement reached with another department, a submission to an independent or parliamentary committee, or in a bill or statutory instrument. Ministerial approval for the final product is relatively easily described: the minister simply 'signs off' on it—indicates approval of or, in the guarded terminology of UK government, 'contentment' with, the proposed document or action. Less straightforward is the quest for ministerial guidance *before* the end result of the policy work is approved. Given that ministerial guidance is often vague at the early stages of policy development, it is not always easy to know what a minister wants with regard to the specific applied issues on which a policy official may be working. The procedures for getting ministerial guidance in such circumstances through the notion of the 'steer' is a further key method of maintaining ministerial control over a process in which both ministerial knowledge and direct command are limited.

This chapter looks at the ways policy officials exercise their discretion. The environment in which discretion is exercised is generally one of informality. While the authority of ministers and senior officials remains unchallenged, relations between middle-ranking policy officials and their political and administrative superiors do not tend to be restricted in form, content, or style to following what might be expected to be formal lines—approaching ministers or very top officials only through immediate superiors, only acting on the basis of explicit superior approval, and conducting formal meetings with senior officials. We move on to look at the relationship between middle-ranking policy officials and ministers, including the relationship with those supporting the minister—the minister's private office and special advisers. Senior officials also help shape the work of middle-ranking officials, but usually in a rather indirect and informal way. Given that direct instruction from ministers and top officials offers middle-ranking officials little guidance over how they should work, we look at the cues middle-ranking officials use to orient their work and highlight the importance of the concept of 'steer' as a means of exercising authority in this relatively informal world.

## Informality

While this book is centrally concerned with the relationship between hierarchy and expertise, Whitehall departments are not overtly hierarchical places in which to work. The most obvious sign of this absence of formality to the outsider is the general impression respondents give of working in an atmosphere of solidarity with everyone collaborating with team spirit in a collective effort. In such collaboration differences in grade are respected, but do not shape interactions. In one case, a project that involved close collaboration between different departments, the Grade 7 describes the involvement of even junior staff (EOs):

Everybody worked on the report. There were five areas [of this policy that we looked at], one person took responsibility for each area. When one person responsible for the area went [and spoke to people in the field or in other departments to develop ideas for the policy], they would always be accompanied by another member of the team. I had one area, the HEOs and SEOs [in the team] had other ones, the other Grade 7 and the Grade 5 gave support but did not have responsibility for an area.... I was the most senior person with an area so I was an exemplar for the others.... It was very much a team effort. The EOs would be accompanied by a Grade 7. We wanted them to get a lot out of it and make it theirs.

An HEO described her work:

Does the Grade 7 take a close look at what I do? It depends on the Grade 7. Daphne is quite a hands-on person and is more than fully aware of what we are doing. Drafts are passed on to her and she has made comments 'you need to do such and such' or 'speak to someone about this' before it goes out. This is a team, grade is not all that relevant—of course it has some relevance sometimes, but we mostly work together as a team.

As this quote indicates, and as will be elaborated further, grades generally make a difference, but not in the sense of any rigid demarcation between the types of jobs that can be done or in any formalities to be observed in channels of communications.

An official from the successor to a department that had the reputation of being more hierarchical in its approach, the old MAFF, displayed the only case that came close to Gouldner's (1954) 'punishment-centred' bureaucracy. A DEFRA official working in a job that was formerly exercised within the MAFF saw senior involvement and oversight as a response to a lack of confidence in middle-ranking officials:

My old Grade 5 used to get involved a lot in things that I did, but that was only until he felt confident that I could do things. Heads of department have to be confident, if in doubt, they'll dabble. My current Grade 5 will dabble. Luckily he trusts me enough not to. Others feel he dabbles too much, but that is probably because they have not done enough to get his trust. They maybe need to concentrate on that instead of complaining about it. John is a hands-on sort.

The distinctiveness of MAFF may also help explain why the Phillips Report on the Bovine Spongiform Encephalopathy (BSE) crisis of the 1980s and 1990s found a more hierarchical structure in the part of MAFF dealing with animal health than we generally found in other departments (see Phillips 2000: vol. 15, pp. 9–10). Even from the perspective of other parts of MAFF, things looked different. A Grade 7 argued:

MAFF was an incredibly hierarchical place. There is a hierarchy there now, but I would say it is an empowered hierarchy. My HEOs do briefings and meet the minister. They send things to me, but they don't expect me to intervene unless they want me to. I like to think that I have a clear idea of what they are doing, and what sort of workload they have at any time, and know when they are overloaded. It is a bit like the relationship I have with the Grade 5. The Grade 5 will ask me to do something and leave me to do it. But he will help me if I am stuck. I won't expect him to dot every 'i' and cross every 't'. The system gives people space up and down and laterally.

And an SEO from MAFF also argued:

> The way the department works is that we are moving away from gradist stratification. [Jane, the Grade 7] and I are probably good advocates of moving that way—working towards a project basis of working. We split the work in terms of priorities and availability to do it. I have been doing a composite job similar to Jane's but in other areas.

There was a handful of examples of 'gradist stratification' in patterns of communication and responsibility in other departments, but these were rather rare among our respondents. As we will see, even the tendency to show things to superiors before sending them to the minister has less to do with observing formality than with seeking the kind of guidance that colleagues, peers as well as superiors, can offer.

## Dealing with the minister

### The minister

Informal patterns of relations within ministries are not only found among officials. We came across rather informal relations between middle-ranking officials and ministers as well. One does not have to be in the SCS to meet a minister. If a minister wants to know something—be briefed or kept up to speed on what is going on with a particular initiative—he or she will meet the person who can help directly. A Grade 7 illustrated his relationship by recalling some recent banter with his minister:

> Yes I have a lot of contact with the minister—the other day, I saw him, last Thursday after the reshuffle, I asked him, 'Have you heard from Number 10 yet?' He said, 'Get away you cheeky bugger'. We get on well. It is the same with most people in the directorate. All of my HEOs have as much contact as I do, and as informal. That is the way I work. Some people keep the ministerial contact for the higher grades. For me, if you do the work, you do the work. There are some issues where I need to take the lead, but otherwise they have contact with the minister.

This respondent's experience of direct meetings with the minister was shared by many others:

[Say, you have] put a submission together that goes in in paper terms [for the minister]. If the minister wants to discuss it, in the old days it would be the Grade 3 that did it, but it is now recognized that the people who wrote the paper should do it. Submissions go forward from SEOs, HEOs, and Grade 7s—it is all different now, thank heavens.

Others tended to see the lack of contact as a matter of ministerial style rather than any general feature of a hierarchy:

Contact with the minister? A lot depends on ministers. The ministers here don't have as much personal contact as we had with ministers in my previous post. When I was working on domestic violence I saw the minister frequently. Now much of the contact is through submissions and contact with the private office. You put something in and they tell you the minister accepts point 1 but not 2 or 3 and such like.

For others the frequency of ministerial contact depends on the nature of the task. Contact with interest groups, though often direct, may be mediated by the minister over especially sensitive issues: '[*Interviewer: Did you see the people from the major interest group opposed to the measures you were proposing?*] You usually see them in the minister's office, I did not go to see them [on my own].' Legislation going through parliament may involve officials in frequent contact with the ministers responsible. A Grade 7 responsible for a sensitive bill describes its parliamentary stages:

We were continually bringing ministers in. In [late] 2001 and end of the bill, while parliament was in session, I saw minister once a day. It was absolutely central. We had different things to say to the minister at different times—what he would say in parliament tomorrow, effectively, and that would be different things depending on whether it was the second reading or discussion on amendments. We approached him with policy development decisions. As it was going through there were still issues to be resolved and new bits to the bill, and some structural suggestions made by the stakeholders. We made policy submissions to him on that and spoke to him at the same time.

Respondents doing bill work were the most likely to report frequent contact with the minister apart from those working in a private office. Contact with the minister is not necessarily a desired activity. A Grade 7, for example, said:

I have contact with [the minister of state] every couple of months. It depends on what is going on. I don't always want to go. There was a press briefing last week as we published a [policy] paper. I sent Fredericka [an HEO] along—I could have gone but did not. He [the minister] does all the talking. When he asks the official a question it is always the question you don't know the answer to, so I left that to Fredericka.

We will return to the role of the minister in directing the work of the civil servant later. Meanwhile, relationships between middle-level policy bureaucrats and ministers are not hierarchical in the sense of ministers being a source of instructions, which filter down to them through the upper reaches of the bureaucracy. Ministers can be, and are, approached and contacted by middle-level officials. Policy work does not generally bring such officials daily or weekly in contact with ministers, but contact can be frequent and direct under some circumstances.

## Private office

While many middle-ranking officials indicated they had direct meetings with the minister, most of the contact with the minister for all grades, even senior grades, takes place through private office: the group of civil servants who pass things on to a minister (described in Chapter 3). An SEO working on a minister's pet scheme pointed out:

When you do something like that, it is surprising how much contact you have with the minister's private office. Whether this is a recent change in style or whether it is down to one minister I am not sure. With [the current minister of state] you even get emails direct without them being filtered through his private office. But I was getting emails two to three times a week from his private office too.

On a few occasions respondents referred to hierarchical formalities in these communications. An HEO within the DfES, not noted for its adherence to hierarchical formalities, said:

I have not personally referred things to private office but given it to the range 10 [equivalent to Grade 7] or the Grade 5 to send up to them. If it is a standard PQ [Parliamentary Question], I might send that directly to private office.

However, from the point of view of private office, contact with people in the policy sections of the department generally means contact with a Grade 7 primarily because they tend to 'lead' on a particular issue (i.e. they have responsibility for, and know about, it). A private secretary in the office of a minister of state described her contacts with the departments:

Yes, you get to know people, and it is important that you do. When something negative happens you need advice. If you have a working relationship with the people who lead on issues, and they might be Grade 7 or Grade 5 (or even possibly higher), you get advice much more quickly than if you send a letter to someone you don't recognize. From their side, if there is someone in private office they can phone up and ask something that saves them a lot of time and effort, and you are that link.

Moreover, the link between the minister and workers in a private office can be close: one HEO(D) told of a working weekend spent at a minister's family home, along with another Cabinet minister, and another official in a private office commented: 'There is a high level of trust between the minister and the private secretary, and she will talk to me more openly than to other civil servants.'

The importance of private office as a channel for communication with the minister means most communications sent from officials to the minister are written, despite the possibility of face-to-face contact. Written communications passed to the minister are of three broad kinds: briefings, submissions, and papers, in descending order of frequency mentioned in the interviews. *Briefings* cover key issues in existing policy or outline the details of new policy. Thus, one official responsible for NHS income generation argued that ministers need briefings on the 'unusual things like the libyan sextuplets case last year'—referring to the case of a Libyan woman who gave birth to sextuplets while visiting Britain at a cost cited in newspapers as £500,000 (see 'Libyan couple "will pay NHS bill for births" ', *Daily Telegraph* 20 August 2001)—as well as new policies such as charges for hospital treatment for road traffic accident victims. As she put it:

> We are just doing a consultation on charges under the Road Traffic Act. These will be substantially raised, and there will be articles in the *Daily Mail*... complaining about a stealth tax. As part of the briefing we will anticipate this and set out the lines to take on them.

Briefings for ministers responsible for taking bills through parliament produce lengthy documents, with some respondents reporting briefings of over 500 pages, which have to be carefully laid out and indexed so ministers can access briefings on individual clauses and issues.

*Submissions* set out proposed courses for action, usually requesting some kind of 'steer' or approval. An official working on a bill described the nature of submissions she sent to the minister:

> In the submission we would outline what the issue was, say something like 'we could go two ways on this' and give options, but we always made sure we made a recommendation. There was lots of detail that we worked out ourselves without sending it to the minister. It seemed like we were taking decisions as we went along, but we would always send it up at some stage. Some technical detail we did not check with Private Office.

Another official working on a bill offered a slightly more open-ended submission (although, as we will see later, much preparatory work is done before a 'steer' is usually requested):

> At [this particular stage in policy development]... there were two major policy submissions on this issue. In October 2000 when we worked out the bare bones of the scheme and put it to the Home Secretary for comments. The sort of thing we put forward was 'here is how we think it will work—what do you think of it?' rather than options. With more time we might have come up with options. With the Human Rights Act angle this was the only way we could see how this could work.

Submissions could lay out general plans for approval. One official described how the team she was working in proposed to send out possibly sensitive information on the pay of one group of NHS professionals to NHS administrators, and she wrote a submission 'to ministers to say "we want to send this out to the NHS". They said "yes" in principle but they want to see exactly what goes out'.

*Papers* tend to be wider explorations of policy issues that do not necessarily request ministerial approval or direction or any direct reply and as such can sometimes be circulated more widely. A Treasury Grade 7 who wrote a paper on a particular aspect of devolved public finance proposing a new funding mechanism for one part of the budget said: 'I wrote the paper on this and it went to Number 10; although I had copied it to the great and good there was no input at all from them. It became the core document for the scheme.' Although the term 'paper' tended to be used more loosely than 'briefing' or 'submission'—some respondents used the term 'paper' interchangeably with 'submission' and others seemed to use the term for communications with senior officials rather than ministers.

Press offices of ministries can be copied in to submissions and briefings that involve public communication, and can also help shape the minister's reaction. A Grade 7 official spoke of one case:

The review of [a major piece of legislation] . . . started as a small document and became quite large as more specialized issues came into it. . . . This was sent to . . . the new minister. In fact the submission went to him with the document and we asked if he was content to send it out for consultation. The press office thought 'Oh dear, a new minister, there are some sensitive issues in there and if he went out not fully briefed it could be bad', it was, after all, our answer to [a major scandal that hit newspaper headlines some months before]. We will be sending it out for consultation later.

Yet for the most part press offices were mentioned more often by respondents as important contact points over press releases and similar documents rather than places that had to be copied in to submissions, papers, and specialized briefings.

## Special advisers

One curious absence from our interviews with people who dealt with ministers either directly or indirectly on a routine basis was the low frequency of mentions of special advisers. The Blair government has not only increased the number of special advisers but is widely reputed to have seen an increase in their influence within ministries and government as a whole (Select Committee on Public Administration 2001; Wicks Committee 2003). Special advisers were mentioned spontaneously as relevant to the daily work of only seven of our interviews, and two mentions were minor and incidental.[24] Before exploring why advisers seem to make such little impact on the daily lives of policy officials, let us look at the times they were mentioned.

One mention of a special adviser was as a kind of meddler whom one had to accommodate, since his word was effectively that of the minister. The incident related to an official working in a team preparing a complex set of arrangements to measure performance. Since these performance measurement plans required the collaboration and agreement of professional service providers and outside consultants, it took months of careful work and negotiation. Just when the scheme had been settled, a special adviser came along with what to the official concerned seemed to be a fashionable alternative approach to performance measurement. For ease of exposition and to maintain anonymity we may give the approach the fictitious name of 'Dual Focus'. The official told the story:

We had it all sorted and then another interesting angle crept in. [The adviser found a new way of doing things, Dual Focus]. Apparently she got it from a Japanese business philosophy. Something about...a virtual [parallax view]. It was trailed as a phrase 'Dual Focus' and as we speak we are considering Dual Focus measurement.... Yes, we had a blue skies idea here. Not at all clear. We are looking at exactly what 'Dual Focus' might actually mean. It came in overnight. When someone like [this adviser], who has clout and the ear of ministers, comes up with something like this, then it happens very quickly. You can't say 'no', we have to listen. We called an emergency get-together. We brainstormed the initial idea and how it applies to [doing the measurements]. We had to communicate with ministers to get them to agree to this. And there were consequences for other [aspects of our performance assessment]. If we were doing 'Dual Focus' [here], then why not [in other areas]? I was at the stage of [finalizing] the proposal we had worked out with . . . everyone else, and about to get people to sign up to it when 'Dual Focus' came along. It was [the adviser's] influence. Before that the political input we had was from [the junior minister] who just said that she wanted the [people to be able to fill in the necessary forms] online.

The official went on to describe how his team used 'Dual Focus' to help him and his colleagues solve another problem they had experienced under the plans it replaced. In the other six spontaneous mentions of special advisers they were seen as close associates of the minister. In two, both from the ODPM, advisers were mentioned only in passing ('once we reach the next stage in developing this policy we will have a meeting and the minister will have an adviser in with him' and the vaguer 'ministers look to special advisers for advice'). But four of the respondents from the Treasury indicated an altogether stronger role for advisers in their policy work. In the Treasury contact with the minister was likely to be mediated by special advisers: while this was found in only four of the ten interviews in the Treasury, it was found in no other department as such a regular feature of policy work. When one ODPM Grade 7 was asked if he had contact with special advisers, he replied: 'Not at my level. The Grade 3 does and the press office types.' A Grade 7 in the Treasury, however, argued:

We don't get to see ministers all that much, so special advisers are quite important. We work with them, especially when the issue is a topical one. Yes, they can give a clear steer. How often we meet them is issue-driven. We may have nothing for two or three months and then they want to know what you are doing and get involved. Yes, they can initiate contacts.

Another stated briefly in response to a question about contact with ministers: 'I deal directly with special advisers—Ed Balls. And Gus O'Donnell [the permanent secretary]. I talk directly to special advisers.' This evidence suggests that in these cases a role for special advisers is equivalent in some respects to that of a junior minister in other departments, especially through their authority to give a 'steer'. While it would be a mistake to argue that advisers have an especially prominent role in the Treasury simply on the basis of a handful of spontaneous mentions of the role in a non-random sample, such a view fits other descriptions of the operation of the Treasury under Chancellor Gordon Brown, and especially the role of Ed Balls as his special adviser between 1997 and 2004 (see Thain 2002, 2004).[25] When prompted about the role of special advisers, a fast streamer in a private office argued:

Some special advisers are more high profile than others. In the three years I worked as a policy official I never had contact with them. I put 'SpAds' [a short form for 'Special Advisers'] at the 'copy to' part of anything I sent to the minister. But I was never in that high-profile an area that would merit their intervention. But there are some areas that come up where they are crucial, especially when it comes to brokering agreements with other departments.

The official pointed out that special advisers tended to have functions linked to the mobilization and use of political authority—getting authorization for a deal between departments, especially when there is a time pressure, 'beefing up' speeches or letters written for ministers by civil servants and high-profile contacts with the media. These overtly political roles were not necessarily in competition with civil service roles. Indeed it could be useful to have someone with political authority, albeit secondhand, to be able to deal with issues when the minister was away or unavailable. Moreover, this official suggested advisers had their own paths for contacting ministers:

There are different ways the SpAd might feed stuff to the minister. If I have a submission and if the SpAd wants to comment on it, I'd get in touch and say: 'Fred, here is the submission—do you want to say something?' Sometimes Fred [picks up something going on in the department and] comes to me and says: 'I've seen this, make sure the Secretary of State knows about it.' And he also speaks to him directly. They have weekly meetings. . . . He would not put something directly in the box for the minister [referring to the box of materials put together for the minister to take home to work on]. He would feed it through me, or put it directly to him. But if it were a sensitive issue I would hope it could be discussed before it is put to the minister.

This relationship contains a latent tension. This tension came spectacularly to the fore in the old Department of Transport in early 2002 when disagreements between a special adviser (Jo Moore) and the head of the department's press office (Martin Sixsmith) not only cost both their jobs but also led to the resignation of the Secretary of State, Stephen Byers, and the movement of its permanent secretary, Richard Mottram, to another department (Select Committee on Public Administration 2002). The relationship between minister and adviser is likely to be highly personal. An official not directly involved commented:

Whether the relationship is good or bad depends very much on the individual. [From what I can gather from people who were there, there were no tears shed when one particular adviser left another department]. [This one] was regarded as arrogant and unpleasant. But for the rest you tend to get mixed reports: some say they are helpful, while others don't. A typical criticism of a special adviser is that they don't understand the detail. They are interested in the spin. They have no grasp of the issue yet they come in with a politicized take on it. And advisers say that officials cannot see how things will go down with the outside world.

Thus, while we cannot comment on the wider importance of advisers within a ministry, as a direct source of instructions for policy bureaucrats, their role appears to be more limited than one might at first expect.

## The role of bureaucratic superiors

Senior officials do not generally oversee the work of middle-ranking officials closely. Respondents tended to describe their immediate SCS superiors as either somewhat remote figures or as people one saw all the time and could talk to, but rarely as someone supervising their activities. For those who regarded their Grade 5 as remote, one reason offered for this remoteness is that

Grade 5s typically have a wide range of responsibilities and cannot be closely involved in the work of them all. As a Grade 7 put it:

The Grade 5 does not interfere in what I do at all. What I do is not as sexy as other parts of the division. The whole area is under-resourced. He has to spread himself thinly. He has his nose in slightly higher profile stuff like the Licensing Bill. He leaves me alone and I like the autonomy.

Another frequently cited reason for the lack of SCS involvement in the work of officials at Grade 7 level and below is that they do not have the technical expertise to understand the work they do. One Grade 7 argued that he contacted his Grade 5 a lot, 'but some of the stuff I put to him I'm sure he doesn't understand'. And an HEO argued:

I am an HEO—we do the donkey work. We do all the preparation work for the divisional manager; wherever I have worked I have found divisional managers are happy to take on the views of people down below. . . . You are dealing with a level of detail they don't understand. It is a matter of keeping your eye on the ball at this level and warning senior people if something comes up—if there are any clashes on the horizon. It also means doing preparation. That is how I'd describe myself—and making sure people keep their eye on the ball.

A Grade 7 in the DoH echoed this when she said that she 'tended not to refer matters upwards [to the Grade 5] as knowledge on this was rather limited—it was accepted that there was not much expertise on this', and added that 'the director also had meetings at the director level, but these did not tend to go into detail'.

For those who saw their Grade 5s more often, the spirit in which they met was not of superior–subordinate but of a more collegial team membership. A Grade 7 explained, over a commercially sensitive piece of legislation:

On [this] issue I was dealing more often with the Director (Grade 3). This was sensitive stuff. Yes I can have direct contact with the Grade 3—I could and did involve Mike [the Grade 5] in those developments. I did not have to go through the Grade 5 first. This is not a hierarchical set-up. I very much like to talk to Mike. I have a great respect for who he is and what he does. But this is not a hierarchy thing.

A Grade 7 from HM Treasury replied in answer to a question about the nature of contacts with his Grade 5:

Contact with the Grade 5? I have constant hour-by-hour contact. We're not all in separate cubicles. When I want to talk to her about things, I do, and we also meet regularly. We do have formal meetings too. When you are making policy decisions you need that. You talk to her to share opinions. We all talk to each other, you can't do this job in isolation. We have built up a team which works on team effort and we're not all that grade conscious.

And a Grade 7 from the Home Office working on a politically sensitive issue said:

[How do I relate to my head of unit?] It all depends on the person and the trust and the nature of the working relationship between you. I moved here along with the same guy I used to work for in my old job. I'll generally do my own thing but copy him into the things I am doing. You'll come in and be hit with a load of requests from Number 10. I always copy him into that so he knows what is going on. I might consult him on how he would handle an issue. Once you've done it once or twice you get to know when to run things past him.

Another pointed out that his particular unit had experienced a change from a rather aloof Grade 5 to a more involved and amenable superior:

We have got a new head of division in post. We had a rocky relationship with the previous one. There was a problem about whether the last one had the inclination to find out what we were talking about. The new one is a vast improvement. It was a problem because we were limited in what we could put to him and what he would support us on. The new Grade 5 is picking things up very well. This new one is very much the new type of SCS that people are talking about.

Senior officials tend to be mentioned as people who serve three functions. First, as an 'extra pair of eyes' to look at the work being done within a particular unit, although some send them everything and get little back—in the words of one Grade 7: 'I email things to my manager every hour. I'm not sure whether she actually reads very much of it.' A DEFRA Grade 7 spoke of how she handled a draft submission on an interdepartmental matter:

My HEO drafts it and I'll look at it and send it round and back, discuss it with the divisional manager (Alison, but she is on holiday at the moment). She'll see it anyway before it goes to [the Minister of State] and then it will go round to other ministers for clearance. We'll have copied it around at official level.

Another said he would 'show him [the Grade 5] a draft of a submission before I write it up for his advice rather than approval'. This sentiment was very commonly expressed.

Second, senior officials were especially good at linking the work of those at Grade 7 and below with the 'wider picture', by which was usually meant the cross-departmental perspective or issues of party political sensitivity. Possibly they might take responsibility for a key political area, though only one example was mentioned in the interviews, when an official in the DoH described his work:

We are on the policy development side—the Royal Liverpool Hospitals retention of organs scandal. The Chief Medical Officer produced a document giving advice on the Removal, Retention, and Use of Human Organs in 2001, our Head of Clinical Quality, Ethics, and Genetics..., a Grade 3, did the work on organ retention following on from that in the department.... The review of the Human Tissues Act...was worked on by the Grade 5. [The work expanded as additional issues were raised] such as stem cell and foetal tissue among other things.

More commonly they provide a valuable 'high policy' or political contribution to the work of middle-ranking officials. As an SEO in the DfES put it, 'they are also good at linking politics to what is going on in the department'. A Grade 7 working on a key manifesto commitment, interviewed together with his Grade 5, argued that some of the issues on which he had to write submissions to ministers

were sensitive and I'd send a copy in advance or talk to Phil [the Grade 5] about how to handle it. Routine briefing to the minister was sent straight up uncleared. That was not always the way it went. Even policy development submissions were not always sent round before they were sent to the minister.

His Grade 5 chipped in:

The complexity of the policy work meant that the policy work had to be divided up, so there was a limited degree to which other people working on the bill [apart from the individual dealing with the matter] would be able to say anything about it anyway.

Third, senior officials are necessary sources of authority. Respondents suggested that if a submission were to need extra *gravitas*, or if they were facing a potentially sticky meeting, perhaps arranging a deal with another ministry, it would pay to bring along a member of the SCS—'a Grade 5 makes them get the message' as one Grade 7 put it. Another from DEFRA made a similar point: 'The Grade 5 can be called on to come into meetings and have conversations with our contacts. This would happen with more important things or things with difficulty—he'll add weight.' Even more senior people within SCS can add greater urgency, as a Grade 7 whose policy brief involved getting another department to collaborate with it suggested:

We want to get the Grade 3s there at the meeting [with the other department] as we hope they will come along to speak for [our] whole department in policy terms.... And...if we ask [someone to do something within the other department we are dealing with] there is the authorization and they can say to people in their department that the Grade 3 sanctioned it. It gives it a sense of urgency too with a Grade 3.

Or senior officials may step in to save the day when a junior official is outgunned or outmanoeuvred in intradepartmental negotiations, as a Grade 7 in DfES responsible for a particular set of subjects within the school education system put it:

Once we come up with the recommendations, that might be conflictual—[we will hear from all the other subjects and we will discuss] whether there should be more teachers in MFL [Modern Foreign Languages] and all the other interests in the department after more resources [will make their case]. [*Interviewer: Will you get to argue the resources case for the subject areas you are responsible for?*] Yes, I expect I will get to argue it within the Department. If I'm losing the argument or making a hash of it, I expect my manager will probably step in.

An HEO(D) managed to create a new noun out of her Grade 5:

On my European job—I am in a team but I'm the one responsible for the Green Paper work. I work to a Grade 7 but I am doing it. At the end of April some representatives of other government departments—the DfES, the Cabinet Office, the DWP, the Treasury, the Small Business Service of the DTI, and the DTI—got together and brainstormed ideas about what should be in it. The people there were up to Grade 7, there was not much *Grade 5-ness* going on there, except for our Grade 5 [who was there].

By this she meant that the meeting did not produce any significant interdepartmental commitments. However, one official, an HEO(D), suggested that the line between Grade 7 and Grade 5 responsibilities may not be hard and fast, although for interdepartmental relations it is usual to match grade for grade at meetings where one does not want to be outgunned.

When we met with the Treasury we had a Treasury Grade 5 [at the meeting] who works with the [Treasury] Grade 7. The Grade 5 left to work somewhere else so we only deal with the Grade 7, and only the Grade 7 comes now. There were *big* policy issues concerned.

Moreover, that bill teams preparing major primary legislation for parliament are frequently headed either by a Grade 7 or a Grade 5, and that we came across several reports of Grade 5s 'doing Grade 7 jobs', suggest that the level of responsibility can occasionally be somewhat blurred at this level.

Bureaucratic superiors, above all those in the SCS, have an important role in supervising the work of those below them. However, their roles only rarely involved directly looking over the shoulder and directing or nudging the work of subordinates in directions they thought they should be going. Like ministers, senior officials do not usually stand over their middle-ranking policy officials. As one Grade 7, a frequent visitor to Brussels dealing with the implementation and reform of an EU regulation central to allowing the mobility of labour, put it:

At the end of each presidency there will be a meeting of social security ministers. The Grade 3s and 5s will accompany the Secretary of State, but they certainly do not look over my shoulder at what is going on. If I thought they wanted to know something I'd send an email.

Administrative superiors are important sources of advice and authority. But they make rather rare appearances in our interviews as sources of direction about how middle-ranking officials should exercise their discretion. How, then, do policy bureaucrats exercise their discretion?

## Cues and discretion

Ministers tend not to issue direct and clear instructions to policy officials that define what they should do with any precision, and senior officials tend to offer advice and support rather than commands and injunctions. While they are subordinates within departments, middle-ranking policy officials exercise discretion. Contemporary theories of administrative behaviour tend to assume that administrative discretion is found where formal rules and relations are silent and allows officials to exercise their own preferences. These preferences might be shaped by background or socialization (as with 'representative bureaucracy') or they may arise from some form of self-interest. Such self-interest may be reflected in the pursuit of material benefits (as in rational choice theory, see Niskanen 1971) or of other personal goals such as status, self-esteem, or an agreeable working environment (Downs 1967; Dunleavy 1991). While almost any action, including extreme altruism, could be reframed as the product of self-interest, the term is indiscriminate and it does not help us in practice to understand the exercise of discretion in this way.

Policy officials did not indicate that they *felt* they had substantial discretion. Yet discretion is not the same as independence from hierarchical measures—such as the application of rules or of the direct authority that comes from seniority—but is exercised where such measures are *not directly applied*. Since authority and hierarchy are ever present, even though seldom applied, it is understandable that officials might not perceive themselves as having much freedom to determine the content of policy. Officials know that any significant policy initiatives, or even any significant features of policy initiatives, either need to be sanctioned by ministers or have to be treated as if they were subject to being sanctioned by ministers. The timing and logistics of such sanctioning can at times be problematic and will be discussed later. Discretion is exercised within this context of ministerial sanctioning—actual, deemed, or anticipated—and this context shapes the way policy officials think about their work. Policy officials bend over backwards to produce policies consistent with what ministers want. As the BSE inquiry (Phillips 2000: vol 15, p. 10) noted:

Mr Alistair Cruickshank [a Grade 3 at the time] of MAFF's Animal Health Group told the Inquiry that the advice given by officials to Ministers would often be affected to some degree by their understanding of the Minister's current thinking. He commented, 'It is entirely normal for officials to shade their advice to Ministers in this way: there is no point whatsoever in putting forward advice which has very little chance of being accepted'.

The central difficulty with bending over backwards to make sure you produce something the minister is going to approve of has already been suggested: ministers often have few clear ideas about what they want at the level of the specifics. In the absence of any clear direction about what to do, officials have to rely on a variety of cues that indicate the direction in which they should develop policies. For the most part these cues are not very difficult for officials to detect.

1. *The perceived 'thrust' of government policy.* Governments have thrusts of policy that can be used by officials as indicators of what ministers want. In an earlier work, Page (2001: 71–2) showed how broad themes such as deregulation and privatization could

be used to guide officials in developing policy. It is also possible for more specific thrusts to be detected as guides. An official working on changing rules for recruiting medical personnel from abroad argued:

Then we went into discussion with the Joint Committee about streamlining. We knew this is what ministers want. [*Interviewer: Did you find this out through private office?*] No there was no direct reaction from ministers' private office—this only went to ministers as part of wider briefing. We knew this is what they wanted through the clear priority given to the need to recruit more doctors. If the system gives the perception that doctors are being regulated out of being recruited then we have to change this as it is damaging.

The perceived thrust of government policy was especially important, although not the only cue, for one official faced with the task of interpreting the diverse responses to a government consultation document. When writing a report on the consultation for his minister he said:

You give weight to things that are related to political priorities. If ministers want you to reduce teacher burdens, and something comes up in the consultation that says burdens will be increased or decreased, you highlight this as evidence of an effect on teacher burdens, even if only one person has said it. Then you give extra weighting to some organizations rather than others—the Local Government Association is a big organization and what they say is usually worth reporting. That's the way it is. After that you pull out the points made most frequently. And of course you highlight the things that make a good news story.

Moreover, officials will look hard for cues about what they think the thrust of government policy is in their particular area. An official working on waste disposal described how he went about his work:

We have responsibility for the recommendation about charging householders for waste disposal [and the pilot schemes resulting from that]. . . . The Government said it could not make its mind up . . . and needed further work and would decide later. What was said specifically in that case was that they would look at the research in other countries. They would see if fly-tipping increased, whether it had a disproportional impact on those with low incomes, whether it was costly to administer, and so on. This gives us an idea of what we need to look at.

Another Grade 7 official leading a bill team was involved in the work of the PIU, which developed New Labour ideas on the 'modernization' of this particular policy, and this association with New Labour thinking helped him in writing the legislation: '[O]n the modernizing agenda [this experience helped in] understanding where the government was coming from.' Officials will look to a variety of statements, precedents, or other indicators to try to determine the general thrust behind the policy they can then use in shaping it.

2. *Experience from frequent interaction.* Some officials in frequent contact with a minister get to know the way a minister thinks and base their judgements on this experience. Most obviously such experience was the basis on which all officials in private office suggested they knew what among the many items sent up from the department by way of submissions the minister did or did not want to see. We have already noted how officials in private office observe how a minister's 'interests develop' and learn through experience to form judgements about what a particular minister will want to have passed on to him or her and what does not need to be drawn to his or her attention. Yet familiarity with the minister is not the sole preserve of officials in private office. Officials generally experienced more contact with ministers in dealing with issues they referred to as 'sexy' or 'topical', or matters that ministers made a personal point of getting involved in. On one such topical issue, the official, a Grade 7, argued:

Once we get a definite proposal we want to put forward we go to [the Minister of State] and have lots of meetings with him. . . . [I]n preparing and going to those meetings you get an idea of what is on the minister's mind, and in drafting speeches for them. Their reactions to the speeches and the changes they make and the discussions about it. Every now and then sitting in the car you get to chat informally. In the past seven or eight months I have met him four or five times.

A Grade 7 who represents her department in Brussels said, in response to the question of how it is possible to know what line ministers would want her to take in EU negotiations:

On more important issues we'd go to ministers for advice. Or when we send them a report back after a meeting they may want to see us if they have anything they want to discuss. I've enough experience on this and I've rarely been taken by surprise about what position they want us to represent.

A slightly different gauging of the mind of the minister can come from trying to think oneself into the position of the minister, as suggested by an official writing a paper proposing policy options in a social welfare issue who felt he knew what the minister was likely to want by observing her: 'The paper has to be finished tomorrow and will be sent up saying "this is how we want to do the review, do you agree?" The minister gave us no steer but we see where she was coming from and why she had to do it, so we have ideas about the sort of thing we should do.'

3. *Departmental priorities.* Some of the lines officials take when approaching policy development are assumed to be official lines established by departmental practice over years. As one Grade 7 put it:

How do we know what ministers want? At one level if you work in a particular department (I've worked in three) you fairly readily pick up the aims and objectives—the vision if you like. That gives you a starting point.

An obvious example of such priorities can be seen in how departments approach financial issues. In the Treasury, officials responsible for supervising the budgets of spending departments had little difficulty in identifying a departmental view on spending proposals:

If there are issues I am uncertain of I might go to the team leader, but it is fairly clear most of the time what the Treasury position would be. I know what the team's objections would likely be.

A Treasury official responsible for supervising approvals of large items of capital spending in another government department argued:

How do I know the Treasury view? There is a system in place that we have developed with [the spending department] over the years. They send us far in advance their business cases (i.e. the documents used to convince our ministers) so we can identify potential problems. The business case will try to reflect the Treasury view. They will say that the case is based on 'contact with Treasury colleagues and the content reflects this'.

Moreover, this is not simply a Treasury matter. One official responsible for capital finance issues in a spending department argued: 'How do I know what the Treasury view is? I know that they are after wider markets, balance sheets, dispersals, maximizing receipts—all issues I am aware of.' Spending departments generally seek to ensure that their budgets are safeguarded—securing funds from the Treasury for new policy commitments is an important part of policy development. An official in the DoH had no problems identifying a departmental line on income generation in reclaiming health charges from insurance companies for motor accidents:

Here's a recent issue. The Act [concerned] says that you can claim NHS charges where the insurer makes a compensation payment. Now some companies with fleets have a £250,000 excess waiver. So sometimes the owner of the fleet will stump up the money without an insurance claim. A couple of companies said they did not have to pay NHS charges since it is the 'insurer' who pays, and they are not the insurer. We got advice from our solicitors. Then a whole load of companies came out of the woodwork who had similar positions. We went to DETR [which ceased to exist in 2001] for advice. They said that the companies' position was illegal. Excesses could not cover a third party, just yourself. We went to the Insurance Inspectorate at the Treasury. We went to the solicitor who said we should seek counsel. We went back to DETR again who said they would take it further with the insurers. . . . This is big. The thing came to light because of us, and because one company tried to claim they were exempt.

An official from a spending department responsible for providing the UK line on EU issues showed the convergence between the Treasury and spending departments on some issues: '[We] and the Treasury are very close. Our view on the budget dovetails with our view on policy. We will always question any increase in expenditure.'

Departmental priorities could be non-financial. Several of the officials involved in interdepartmental bodies considered themselves as 'representing departmental interests'. An official working on a cross-ministerial bill team stated:

[The main department sponsoring the bill] was worried that [since they were doing bits of the bill that belonged to our department] they had more work to do so they actually wanted help. Ideally they wanted more than one member of staff to come across from [our department]. So it was in both departments' interests. If I had not been over there then [our department's] angle might have been forgotten. The policy people [in my department] could and did contact the bill team—but if they had concerns they could go directly to me. There were also...measures [which were the responsibility of a third department] in the bill. But that was too small to send someone over to the bill.

An official representing his department's line on one particular measure in the EU commented:

Colleagues from DoH and Inland Revenue will be there with us in Brussels. We have our own parochial interests as well as the UK interest to represent. We have [i.e. our department has] the biggest interest.

Yet where ministerial and departmental priorities conflicted, and the minister had expressed a clear view on the matter, there was no question but that the minister's view prevailed. As an HEO working on some new legislation pointed out:

[*Interviewer: Where did the policy come from?*] It came from the ministers. They came to a decision on which way we should jump on this. The route the minister favoured was not the way we suggested. We had to work on this. It was still our view that this was a rather unnecessary additional bit. So we had to work out how to make it work. It could be dealt with more appropriately somewhere else through other means, but it had to be made to work so we were figuring out how to make it work.

4. *Documents*. Documents, not necessarily produced with the involvement of the minister, and not even necessarily government

documents, can be used to guide policy development. A Grade 7 charged with drafting the statutory guidance for charging for local social services described how he did his work:

> How do I work out which things to include in the guidance? Here we were helped by the Audit Commission report. It was a good starting point. We did not before that have information on local charging policies. The Commission did a survey with a very good response rate. This is the first time we had such information. There were also plenty of pointers in the Audit Commission report. It was based on what one authority did—Torbay. It was a go-ahead place. It was also associated with a Cabinet Office 'Learning Loop'.

Another official, involved in developing foster care described how she went about her work:

> There was no direct steer from the minister. We knew the sort of thing that was required by looking at where the impulse comes from—the inspection report on the commissioning of foster care services which was very disappointing. There are a number of factors of which that is the key one. This takes a lot of my time. It also ties in with the education of looked-after children which has been investigated by the Social Exclusion Unit. Partly this will be about how to take the next phase on. This means looking at the interim report and taking part in their formal meetings.

An official in the DTI who was working on the reform of competition policy described how he did his work:

> We get the recommendation from the Office of Fair Trading report, I draft a submission setting out what it says and then a recommendation on how to deal with it and cover matters of handling and timing. I or a person I work with drafts a submission, we will do it in consultation with my boss. She does the corrections to the first draft and sends it to the minister.

5. *Consensus mongering.* UK civil servants have been described as 'consensus mongers' (Rose 1981) with the 'preferred policy style' of negotiating a consensual solution to a problem (Jordan and Richardson 1982). While finding a consensus among different views was not a common means of determining what policy should be, it was used in some contentious policy issues. An official working for the NHS argued:

My job is going out talking to people. I could write the policy myself, but it would not have much credence. Lots of training workforce development confederations—groups of employers that cover geographical areas, there are 28 of them, made up of key members of the local healthcare economy: trusts, higher education institutions, social services.

An official dealing with NHS policy was concerned with developing a new scheme for medical staff remuneration and indicated that failure to reach agreement could hold up policy development:

I have been looking at [a new] scheme [for nearly a year]. I arrived when a consultation document had been sent out on the scheme. We needed to turn the outcome of the consultation into a new scheme. This has involved putting submissions to ministers on the outcomes of the consultation, getting steers from ministers, especially in areas where the consultation was (often deliberately) somewhat vague, and making sure it all ties in with the timing for the implementation of the new...contracts. It is all about...clearing lines of consultation with ministers, the Chief Medical Officer and engaging with the BMA and trying to get them signed up with what we want to do. And we have to deal with the other stakeholders—the [relevant] advisory committee...an NDPB. We've not made an awful lot of progress.... [Some of these people have been dragging their feet and one of the stakeholders] did not even want to give us a date when we could meet and talk about this, I think for tactical reasons. So a lot of my job of late has been trying to keep this thing moving....Now we need to get a date to start dealing with these issues and [one of the interest groups involved] is playing silly buggers with the dates again.

In both these and similar cases, consensus mongering was less a solution devised by the policy official as a means of developing policy and more an activity that went with a particular job, which by its very nature—ascertaining the views of others—requires it. Or the search for consensus could be mandated by politicians. As one official involved in the Adoption Bill 2002 pointed out:

The Bill got sent to a Special Standing Committee, which had three public evidence sessions. So we had two public consultations altogether and all

the evidence. That was helpful for the passage of the Bill. The Secretary of State and the Prime Minister wanted it to be [a] cross-party [bill] so they could know what people wanted and show they had consulted. It was supposed to be a consensus bill.[26] It meant that the government could claim that it has met the obligation to listen—we were able to listen to what people said too. A lot of the time managers of the legislative programme do not encourage you to add new bits to reintroduced legislation [following consultation], but we could. We had two set-piece consultations. It was a lot of work. Even physically exhausting.

Officials did not generally see consensus brokering under other circumstances as the proper way to develop policy. When asked whether the financial provisions of a sensitive piece of legislation were developed on the basis of consensus, an HEO said: 'There is consensus within [this] Department.... Whether the [Society representing the major stakeholders] and others like what we do, or the [big voluntary associations], we will need to see.'

## The notion of the 'steer'

One of the most frequently used terms to describe something close to a political directive in policy work is the notion of a 'steer'. We have already used this term as it has come up in quotations discussed earlier, but it needs more consideration since it is a key term used to describe the interaction of political direction and bureaucratic creativity in policy development. As we have seen, ministers rarely give direct instructions (Chapter 4 and earlier in this chapter). The term 'steer' is particularly useful since it acknowledges the superiority of the politician as the person in charge, but is also sufficiently vague, since it is not an instruction. To steer does not require great technical knowledge or technical detail; it implies a more cerebral and strategic activity—as it does in the now popular phrase 'steering not rowing' (Osborne and Gaebler 1992, although use of the term 'steer' in the civil service long predates their work). The term is tactful, as it is not a command and even allows the possibility of questioning the intention behind it without direct conflict.

A 'steer' usually comes from a minister. It may, less frequently, come from a senior official, but its general legitimacy as a guide to developing policy comes because it is directly or indirectly an expression of a minister's wishes. A steer might be given at the start of policy work on any particular issue, as one official working on an elderly care policy project commented, 'We got a clear steer from the outset, so the minister did not need to get back to us as it went along', but such clear initial statements of ministers' wishes that can be used by policy officials to guide their work were not common. Usually steers are incomplete guides to what the official is expected to produce. As one Grade 7 working in a slightly unusual 'blue skies thinking' unit, put it:

The ministerial team, and especially the [Secretary of State], gives a sort of vision and says 'I'm interested in this area' and we take this steer, which is generally very broad, away with us and it is up to us to develop something. We firm up policy ideas.

Such 'steers' are often communicated by word of mouth rather than written (see Chapter 4). Given that it is an informal instruction, it is possible for a steer to offer guidance that would be hard, or at least risky, to put on paper since a formal written instruction may prove potentially embarrassing if it were made public. As one official in charge of a small potentially controversial pilot scheme initiated and publicly announced by a junior minister, who had since moved on to another department, said:

This was not something they wanted to shout about as . . . [it meant that some people were getting a service for free while others had to pay for it]. This was something the [previous] minister at the time really wanted to do, so the steer I got was 'do something along these lines, Brian, but keep it small and keep quiet about it'.

Following a broad initial steer, it is usual to try to determine what the minister wants without going back for more precise indications of what should be done, using the kinds of cues discussed already. While on one occasion we heard that for an elderly care policy proposal a respondent went back to ministers in the early stages of developing policy to ask precisely what they wanted, the norm appears to be to look for as many cues as possible about what the policy work should produce without directly asking the minister. Only once the official has done some work developing options or broad strategies can he or she go back and ask for a 'steer', which generally involves a request for approval of what the official is proposing, a choice between options, or an indication that the work the official is doing is along the 'right lines'. As a high-flyer working on a large bill commented:

In the submission [to the minister] we would outline what the issue was, say something like 'we could go two ways on this' and give options, but we always made sure we made a recommendation. There was lots of detail that we worked out ourselves without sending it to the minister. It seemed like we were taking decisions as we went along, but we would always send it up at some stage. Some technical detail we did not check with private office.

A submission to the minister seeking a steer may also be prompted by the need for approval for a specific action, such as planning a consultation strategy or formally initiating discussions on the issue with another department. But the basic principle is always that as much as possible needs to have been done before the minister is approached. An official responsible for negotiating part of the EU budget, for example, was asked how she knew the line the minister would want her to take.

We don't have authority for a certain amount of money if that is what you mean. But when the problem we are talking about is £200,000 for updating a policy we can be happy that the minister will not want to be concerned and we can decide ourselves. If it is minor, the policy is not controversial and there are no long-term effects that could come and jump back at us, we can decide it. . . . If we are talking about a couple of billions we go to the minister with the pros and cons and ask for a steer, and we'd say 'this is what the Treasury view is likely to be'. Before we go to the minister we will check with the Treasury as we won't want any ministerial correspondence about it.

Doing as much work as possible for the steer is essential—open requests along the lines of 'what do you want me to do?' are not put to ministers. One official about to seek public views on a policy through a consultation summarized tersely the role of ministers:

They make a one-line comment, you come up with a proposal that might be acceptable to them. They say 'I like a and b but not c and d, and we want it in two months'. We say 'yes we can ditch c but are you sure you don't want d because of x'. Once this is clarified you are released to go and talk to the world and his wife about issues and concerns.

Policy officials can obtain a steer from ministers where they are uncertain and request guidance, but they have to do the work first: requests for steers are not open-ended; they take the form of suggestions or options that have to be thought through before they are presented to ministers. At this stage a policy official working on a submission for a steer is most likely to consult an SCS official who also offers advice on such matters as whether the submission is clear, comes at the right time, and addresses the right issues. Discussion with seniors is less a request for formal approval than part of the preparatory work required to ensure that any request is clear and appropriate. As one, more likely to emphasize the role of superiors than most, said:

If I will put up a submission I'll say [to my Grade 5] 'I'm putting a submission up, do you want to look at it?' I might even discuss it with her, her boss, and her boss's boss. If it is bog standard process stuff, then it won't need it, but if it is sensitive, then there is a great facility for testing this out within the Branch.

The same official added, when asked what changes superiors tended to suggest:

The changes are in drafting rather than anything else. You send a half-written submission and say 'shall I carry on along these lines' or you send the whole thing with 'any comments on this? I have to have it in tomorrow'.

Another official, an HEO(D), stressed the informality of the process:

My Grade 7 said 'just do it' [the report I was asked to write on a cross-departmental aspect of industrial policy]. I tend to get the whole thing written before I show her things. My view is that you cannot discuss something if it is not there. She is only a few years older than me and really nice so we can talk quite easily. She reads the draft and she gives comments not so much on the content but on the slant of how it might be made to have greater influence, the political slant on it, and the tactics. If I've had comments and I cannot decide if they are right or wrong she will help.

It is a widely accepted procedural norm that much preliminary work should be done before any submission asking for a steer can be put. An official working in private office said:

[W]hen we receive something from the department we make sure all the material is there we need, we check that it is understandable, and if I can't understand what the submission is about I won't put it before her until I've gone back to them to ask them to clarify. They might send an email—I won't usually ask them to do the whole thing again.

Before ministers are asked to exercise their authority, officials have to have worked hard to prepare a document that has to be clear about what they are asked to exercise it over and in the course of doing so will have often produced proposals in advanced stages of readiness. A 'good submission' to a minister is one that not only makes the substantive case for a particular course of action but also makes the case that the submission is something the minister should read and react to.

## Conclusions

Much of the exercise of authority is invited. Ministers and senior civil servants do not have to instruct middle-ranking policy officials in any detail about what they should be doing. In many cases the injunctions they receive, and the ministerial instructions on which they conduct their policy work, are broad and, in keeping with the general environment of policy work, relatively informal. Senior officials and ministers are generally regarded as not all that interested in the kind of policy detail middle-ranking officials are concerned with, important though it is, and it is for the policy officials working outside the top levels to determine when administrative or political superiors should be involved. As one official working on environmental issues said explicitly:

> Given the technical nature of the job, I have to decide when to involve my bosses and ministers. Much of my work is technical but also potentially very important stuff. Senior people tend not to have time to get into the nitty-gritty stuff, but they are interested in it if it has an impact on wider policy or if it will get media coverage or get stakeholders uptight.

The possibilities for error—things not being passed to the minister that should have been—are large, especially considering that in any one large ministry there are hundreds of people working on policy issues. That no respondents could, when asked, point to a specific mistake in their experience suggests, even if one takes into account they are unlikely to admit errors, that such mistakes do not often come to light. We will comment in the next chapter on the character of 'blame' within the UK policy bureaucracy, but since such errors were generally alluded to in a 'these things happen' tone, they are usually viewed as remediable. One official in a private office answered the question whether he had ever failed to spot things that should have been put to the minister and did not draw them to his attention:

> Sometimes things go wrong, but not too often, or I'd be sacked. The job has a fast pace and priorities change and you get an error rate in all offices. But at the end of the day most situations can be recovered. I have got into situations that could have been handled better, but not had any yet that end in disaster that could not be recovered. Probably the worst that has happened so far is that a decision is taken a bit later than it should have been.

One significant exception to this invited authority pattern is the role of the political advisers in the Treasury who, according to our respondents, are more likely to initiate contacts and take a closer interest in the work of policy officials below the SCS. Yet this tendency should not be overstated, since even here respondents still predominantly described a pattern of invited authority as in other departments.

Rather than officials failing to put important issues to ministers, a more common difficulty of invited authority suggested in the interviews is getting one's invitation accepted—ensuring that superiors, above all ministers, read the submission and give approval or a steer. As a Grade 7 put it: 'You can't expect ministers to grasp things at the technical level. You can't get them to understand, and it delays things.' Another at the same grade explained why his work was taking so long:

You'd have thought that they would have had these all tied up and thrown away by now. Why not? Two issues. Our minister won't sign off the standards because she doesn't have the time to look at them. Ringing the private office every day is a pain for you and for them. Second, the issues cross [departmental boundaries]. You need to ensure that [the other departments] agree in principle, but they are sensitive to the stakeholder provider groups, and they have been infuriatingly slow in getting agreement from their ministers. . . . Our minister is doing a multitude of things. . . . You keep thinking your job is important until you see that of others. Then you realize there are plenty of important things going on.

Another made a similar point about his submission: 'Ministers did not look at it as it was too long and complicated. So we had still not got a policy steer. We had to try and simplify and get them to get their heads around this issue. Yes, they just did not reply to this submission.' On lengthy and complex issues, problems of getting ministers to respond could be exacerbated by the fact that junior ministers move on before the policy is seen through. As a Grade 7 working on a bill argued:

One of the funny things is how many ministers we actually dealt with. . . . [Let me think,] was it seven or eight? More [respondent reeled off a dozen names of ministers]. That will give you an idea of the number of different people we had to brief. We had to bring them up to speed. Some were quicker than others, and some had different ways they liked to be briefed and prepared.

Given this substantial apparent leeway, officials do not regard themselves as having significant policymaking discretion. They know that ministers will at some stage need to approve their actions and exhaust all avenues they believe are available to determine what will be acceptable to the minister. This approach to authority suggests a form of bureaucracy that fits neither a top-down 'punishment-centred' (Gouldner 1954) organization, nor the 'post-Weberian' empowered bureaucracy of the 'reinvented' government model (Osborne and Gaebler 1992), as the authority of the politician has a pervasive impact throughout the policy bureaucracy. Chapter 6 explores the implications of this finding.

# 6

# Controlling Expertise in a Policy Bureaucracy

*r consquently reconsiders, (Clyns protr)*

The empirical picture we have presented of the way a policy bureaucracy works has to some degree challenged prevailing academic
understandings of the way in which middle-ranking officials have
an impact on policy. Their work, far from being subordinate, requires them to develop initiatives, possibly on sensitive topics, and
interact with ministers, senior officials, and those outside the department. Top civil servants are not the only ones to watch if we
want to understand the development of public policy. Moreover,
the empirical picture challenges several prevailing assumptions
about the nature of civil servants at this grade. While in formal
terms it might be possible to point to lower levels of 'competence'—a difficult term usually defined as some blend of individual
aptitude, training, experience, and qualification (see Hood and
Lodge 2004)—simply because such officials are less likely to have a
university degree, in all other respects easy accusations about the
poor 'calibre' of civil servants seem wide of the mark. They can and
do bring to their work imagination, flair, political nous, and an
ability to collaborate with others within the department and
cross-departmentally. Research based on short interviews cannot
establish that they are all as good at their work as each other.
Judging quality of policy work is difficult in general and impossible on the basis of the methodology used here. However, the
interviews revealed no systematic shyness or blinkered or tunnel
vision of the sort one might expect if one were to take seriously the
critiques of the 'hidebound civil service' discussed in Chapter 1.

Moreover, the findings suggest that many of the slick assertions about the character of the civil service and civil servants on which reform is based could be misleading. Our findings suggest that middle-ranking civil servants are open to thinking in a 'joined-up' way and, together with the observation that these officials spend considerable effort trying to follow ministerial initiatives, that any problems of narrow or 'silo mentalities' have at least as much to do with ministerial or SCS approaches to other departments as to any shortcomings in middle-ranking officials. An understanding of the range of tasks involved in developing policy is a much firmer starting point for identifying and remedying any perceived shortcomings in technical expertise and 'competencies' than the kind of broad generalizations about the need for 'delivery', 'change management', and 'leadership' skills that have tended to enter into proposals for reform. To think about effective reform of the roles of the civil service in developing policy, whether reform means making large cuts in the policy bureaucracy or moving officials outside London—to mention two of the big reforms in mid-2004 in the Lyons and Gershon reviews (see Gay 2004)— requires effective diagnosis of perceived problems. Such diagnosis can be based only on an understanding of what it takes to make policy. The boardroom or the top floor might not be the only good vantage point from which to develop an understanding of what needs to change.

Knowing how officials work might help evaluate some of the less visible consequences of reform. One of the implications of the importance of solidarity and feelings of belonging to a collectivity in which the contributions of all grades are appreciated and acknowledged is that some initiatives may weaken or undermine this environment of collaboration and cooperation. We came across expressions of apprehension about the move to a new organizational structure in one ministry, which involved separating 'business design' (close to policy development) from 'project management' (the running of the programme). This apprehension was based in part on the perception that such a separation would be confusing: 'We have to work out where our bit of the job ends and other people's begins. It is not at all clear', as one official commented. In part it came from 'losing ownership'—a dislike of the prospect of losing contact with the other people and issues involved in making a policy work. Above all the separation meant being denied the enjoyment of seeing in action policies one has helped to design, as well as a reduction in one's stake and status in the collective enterprise of policy. Familiarity with how a policy works, albeit gained over a relatively short period, is an important source of expertise, and is at the heart of middle-ranking policy officials' contribution to the policy process. 'The result is that we are not that good at policy any more, and I think we used to be the best department for policy', the official concluded.

However, reform has its own dynamics and logic and it would be unwise to base the case for a better understanding of the work of policy bureaucracies substantially on the implications this understanding may have for reform. Our conclusion explores the implications of our analysis for an understanding of the way bureaucracies work.

## Improvised expertise and invited authority

We can offer a straightforward answer to our question about the relationship between hierarchy and bureaucratic expertise in the UK national government policy process. Returning to the central problem posed by Weber over how it is possible for non-expert politicians to give direction to a specialized permanent bureaucracy, one part of the answer is that expertise is *not subject-based* or technical. Although the majority of our respondents has a university education, it is not essential for policy work at this level. Moreover, it was rare to encounter officials with educational qualifications related to any specific technique or body of expertise on which they could draw in their work. Middle-ranking officials expect to move jobs frequently, and to different types of job, so that the development of expertise in a particular aspect of one policy, or even in one policy field, is rather rare. For an official hoping for career advancement, not necessarily only for advancement to the very top, it is harmful to be a subject specialist. As pointed out in Chapter 2, the most specialized official we came across in our interviews was told to diversify if he wanted to get on. The conventional description of the UK civil servant as a 'generalist' based on an examination of top-level officials also applies much lower down.

The significance of this observation about the lack of subject specialization for our central question is that by minimizing the impact of technical expertise on the bureaucratic policy process, the challenge to hierarchical authority is reduced. Not being a technical expert in the conventional sense means there is less likelihood that a policy official will develop an intellectual or any other attachment to a set of policies, approaches, or ways of looking at a policy problem. The likelihood of policy officials coming up with proposals which have the full authority of a technical expert that challenges politicians' approaches to the same problem is far less than one would expect in a system where technical expertise and subject specialization are high. As Gouldner (1957: 288–9) argued in elaboration of the results of his gypsum mine study, the expert 'is more likely to be oriented to a reference group composed of others, not a part of his employing organization, that is, an "outer" reference group' and hence 'experts are less likely to be committed to their employing organization than to their specialty'.

The second part of the answer to the question of how expertise is handled in a policy bureaucracy is that to a large extent the exercise of authority is invited by the middle-ranking officials themselves. As we saw in Chapters 4 and 5, politicians do not have to spend much time and energy thinking of how to turn their vague ideas into sets of instructions which they then supervise—whether through making sure their top administrative officials use the ministerial hierarchy to ensure the work is done in the way desired, through the activism of political appointees in advisory roles, or through some form of parallel hierarchy such as might be provided by the Treasury, by some of the many units of the Cabinet Office designed to ensure effective performance, or even by organizations reflecting ad hoc initiatives such as the Social Exclusion Unit.

Policy bureaucrats at middle levels are able to take general indicators of ministerial intent and work them into fairly specific proposals or options by using a variety of cues to estimate what the minister is likely to want—to turn straw into spun gold to use the analogy set out at the beginning of Chapter 4. A 'steer' is usually sought only at key stages in the development of policy, often when sets of options have already been formulated. One ex-official, not drawn from our sample, offered the opinion that 'alternatives' are sometimes put in front of the minister so that he or she may feel that a thorough job has been done by the officials and to reinforce the impression that choices are made by the minister even though the officials may have done a good job at elaborating what the minister is likely to want without much direct indication from him or her. Ministerial approval is always required, but it can be given in ways that do not draw ministers into anything like supervision of the policy process.

## Looking through different lenses

### The impact of methodology

How might these conclusions be skewed by the fact that the picture we have presented of this world of policy bureaucracy is a world as seen almost exclusively through the eyes of middle-ranking officials? The argument that academic understanding of the UK civil service has for decades been based upon the similarly potentially skewed perspective of the higher civil service is no proper answer to this question since two wrongs do not make a right. Moreover, we spoke to only a limited number of officials in the SCS, and incidentally (primarily in connection with the study of the work of bill teams, see the Appendix), so we can only speculate on how the research design might have shaped the results. One expectation might be that relatively junior officials overstate their role in the policy process—they make their lives sound more exciting or their jobs more influential than they in fact are. We cannot disprove this hypothesis, but can offer two observations that suggest overstatement by respondents of their role is not likely to be as big a source of bias as might be supposed. First, in three bill teams headed by members of the SCS, the Grade 5s we interviewed gave us pictures of how bills were developed and drafted, including who did what and what importance it had for the overall enterprise, which matched those of the middle-ranking officials exactly. There was no sign of middle-ranking officials seeking to claim great glory and their superiors pulling them back down to size. Second, far from claiming great discretion and influence in shaping the broad contours of policy, middle-ranking officials saw their roles as rather modest. What they can recommend is constrained by what ministers want, or are perceived to want, and they do not consider themselves to have great discretion.

If we consider the world of middle-ranking officials to be that of 'everyday policymaking', and that of ministers and top officials as that of 'high politics', we can come closer to understanding the potential bias of the methodology adopted in this study. Middle-ranking officials do not always have a clear idea of how policy issues, or to be more accurate the policy issues with which they are dealing, are handled in the world of high politics. This observation is not to suggest they have a deficient understanding of policymaking in the UK. When they are given instructions, however vague, to develop a policy, or when something they have suggested finds its way into a manifesto, they can usually offer, if asked, a shrewd guess about how this happened, what political interests were at stake, and who was decisive in moving the issue along. But a common response to a question about what happened in the world of high politics would be speculation about what might have happened along with a recognition that all that is generally known is that a decision 'at a higher level', possibly 'at the highest level' or even 'up there', was taken. The bias of this focus on middle-ranking officials is likely to be less that it overstates their role in the policy process and more that it portrays the two worlds of high and everyday policymaking as touching only when ministers give their steer—a top-down one-way relationship—when in many cases the relationship may be more complex. How the work of middle-ranking officials in everyday policymaking is used by senior officials and politicians to shape thinking about how to develop existing and new policy cannot be gauged by our methodology, and thus we could be overstating the degree of separation between the worlds of high and everyday policymaking.

## Different theoretical perspectives

Might a different set of theoretical propositions have produced a different set of results? The arguments of this book might look familiar to anyone who has followed the *principal-agent* mode of reasoning as a method of analysing public policy. In a nutshell, while politicians do not have all the necessary knowledge and skills to develop a policy, they delegate to an 'agent' (see Kassim and Menon 2002 for a useful introduction and application of the approach to decision-making in the European context). In delegation relationships there are 'information asymmetries' as the principal does not have the knowledge, expertise, or skills of the agent. Moreover, there are conflicts of interest between the principal and agent whose goals may not coincide. As Moe (1984) put it: 'All principal–agent relationships contain within them characteristic agency problems.' Two key agency problems resulting from principal–agent relationships are 'adverse selection' and 'moral hazard' (see Moe 1984; see Kiewiet and McCubbins 1991 for a further discussion of such problems). Because the knowledge of the principal, in this case the politician, is limited, the politician has to rely on selective measures of the faithful implementation of his or her wishes. These measures can only partially assess compliance with the principal's wishes while other aspects of the agent's activity, possibly harmful to the principal's goals and interests, remain unchecked (adverse selection). Moreover, the agents, with their superior knowledge, can evade the control of the principal and 'shirk'—pursue forms of behaviour that suit the agent's rather than the principal's wishes (moral hazard). We have to consider the prospect that this would have offered us a better way of handling our material.

To some extent the theoretical arguments of the principal–agent thesis are not new. The point about information asymmetries was central to Weber's understanding of bureaucracy (1988) and the conflict between hierarchy and knowledge is made explicit in Gouldner's gypsum mine study (1954, 1957) and his related work on cosmopolitan and local social roles. The arguments surrounding adverse selection and to a lesser degree 'shirking' and moral hazard were developed most notably in Merton's analysis (1940) of bureaucratic structure and personality (under the notion of 'overconformity') and Blau's examination (1955) of workers in a state job placement agency. The point here is not to say that others were first, and pointed out similar phenomena long before the attempt to apply the tools of economists to bureaucratic phenomena became fashionable, but rather that using classical theoretical approaches did not make us blind to phenomena that the principal–agent theory would have revealed. Had moral hazard, adverse selection, and shirking been an important part of our story about how hierarchy and expertise coexist within policy bureaucracies, we could have found them using tools available in the tool kit we had chosen to use.

We do not seek to offer a criticism of the whole principal–agent approach in this book. It is a popular approach and we would not want to challenge the belief that it can offer fresh insights into bureaucratic behaviour. We can, however, indicate what we might have found if we had followed the logic of the approach. The approach tends to emphasize formal and structural characteristics of relationships between principals and agents in their handling of the consequences of information asymmetries in formal institutions, such as the delegation to 'independent' agencies, the conditions obtaining in contracts, and the incentives that these formal agreements create. Of course the complexity of the relationship might mean that such contracts themselves are vague 'framing agreements' (Milgrom and Roberts 1992) rather than specific and detailed agreements on mutual obligations. We would probably have had to have developed the outlines of an implicit 'framing agreement' understood by civil servants and ministers. This would be an extraordinarily complex contract as it would involve different levels of ministers (junior and senior), different levels of civil servant (the ranks of hierarchical superiors who could claim some link in the principal–agent chain of our middle-ranking officials), and key institutions such as the Treasury, Cabinet Office, and the private offices of the minister or permanent secretary.

Despite the immense complexity, it may have been possible to develop the outlines of such sets of contractual relationships, but we do not attempt it in our approach to understanding the work of policy officials. Instead we present the trade-off between hierarchy and expertise as sets of norms and expectations about how middle-ranking civil servants behave, how they shape their careers, and how they manage their relations with their administrative and political superiors. Such norms and expectations might have been framed as metaphorical 'contracts' in principal–agent theory. But the only reason, in our view, for attempting this would be a preference for the terminology of the theory rather than additional insight or simplicity of exposition. Arguably to develop such notional contracts would resolve principal–agent theory to a tautology. Contracts, according to the theory, are supposed to provide incentives to certain types of behaviour, and disincentives to others. Where such notional 'contracts' can be constructed on the basis of observed habitual norms and expectations, they cannot also be used to explain such behaviour—one of the main claims of the theory. While this argument does not preclude expressing relationships using the metaphor of contract, it does not offer any pressing reason for doing so, other than a preference for the terminology it employs.

In three important respects, however, we believe that a principal–agent approach could have proved misleading. First, with its emphasis on implementation, the approach would probably have missed the whole area of policy bureaucracy. Instead of delegating policies to agents to carry out, in policy bureaucracies politicians can delegate *policymaking* to middle-ranking officials. Such officials can help shape the goals of policy which might then be passed on to others to carry out. The delegation of policymaking—setting both contours and details of what legislation and other instruments seek to achieve—which the principal can then pass on to another agent is a form of delegation that remains unexplored in the public administration literature.

Second, in its emphasis on patterns of behaviour being created through the specific terms of a contract, the principal-agent approach suggests that different incentives can be created by different contracts. While we cannot claim to have 'explained' the origins of norms that underpin the way policy officials set about their work, and the relationships they form while doing it, such norms appear to be common to so many different departments and contexts throughout the civil service, and in so many different sections and units, that it is inplausible to see such norms as the product of a contract that can be renegotiated, terminated, varied, and even reconstructed *de novo* when the government takes on new tasks or redesigns old ones. Such norms are more likely to have something to do with what it is like to be a civil servant in Whitehall, to pursue a career within its ranks, with observing how others work, and with socialization into the mores of a profession than with incentives created by contract. Moreover, as has been suggested, such norms have such very strong historical continuities, as far as we can tell by reference to Kingsley (1944) and even the Fulton Committee (1968), that to seek to understand them by concentrating on the more immediate circumstances of a contract, notional or otherwise, could be barking up the wrong tree. Rational models of behaviour do not necessarily have particular difficulty with informal rules (Axelrod 1984), but they have not so far featured prominently in the application of such theories to public bureaucracies.

Third, one of the central features of the principal–agent approach is the notion of 'shirking'—the space provided within contractual relations and their supervision that allows agents to pursue their own objectives, possibly at the expense of the principal and his or her objectives. It is quite possible that, given the nature of 'shirking' as something one would not want to boast about for fear of being discovered and being prevented from shirking in future, our research method of short interviews failed to uncover instances of this form of behaviour. Yet our evidence suggests that the absence of direct hierarchical intervention produces another sort of behaviour altogether, and quite the opposite of shirking: the pursuit of cues designed to estimate what the superiors (or 'principals') might reasonably be expected to want. Even if we have underestimated it, shirking does not appear to be an important feature of the world of the middle-level official. The quest for conformity with superiors' wishes, by contrast, is central to this world (see also Kaufman 1960).

Had we approached this study from the perspective of *policy communities and networks*, would it have looked very different (see Rhodes 1997 for an overview)? It would have looked different in a methodological sense because our focus is on individuals, whereas policy community studies tend to focus on collectivities: networks and policy areas. Interpersonal relations are certainly important, but the focus of the approach is on the *interaction between members* of networks and communities rather than the *work of individuals* (see Wilks and Wright 1987). Our concentration has been on the work of middle-ranking officials—sometimes done in collaboration with others, but often in the privacy of their own offices (or frequently their own spaces in a larger open-plan office). We might have found that a study of a particular policy rather than sets of individuals increases the importance of traditional major players for explaining policy outcomes—senior officials, politicians, and interest groups—and diminishes the role played by middle-ranking officials. In some sense this is certain to be true—our focus on policy bureaucrats does not seek to explain why policies take the shape they do, and the role of those not directly covered in this research is certain to be important in any general attempt to explain policy. The fact that our study does not look at these wider influences on policy does not, we suggest, imply that the focus on middle-ranking officials is misleading. The role of middle-ranking officials is not well understood and it is appropriate to understand them as a group before one can think of integrating them into wider network-based accounts of policymaking.

One implication of our finding for the network or communities approach to studying public policy is that many aspects of policy development take place outside networks or communities. This is not only a question of defining some policy areas as subject to influence by networks or communities and others as not. It is quite possible for key decisions that crop up in the process of writing legislation (or otherwise specifying how a policy will work) to be taken effectively by policy officials on their own, albeit within the constraints of what they perceive to be politically acceptable or desirable. Some issues within a policy area might be subject to network/community influence while others might not. This proposition suggests the need for a stronger focus on the agendas of networks if one is to understand their role in the policy process—what issues they get to help decide, what issues are effectively removed from collective discussion and why. A study of networks suggests we look at what networks do. By focusing on middle-ranking officials, we have managed to show that there are important policy issues decided outside them. The difference between issues may in part be the difference between 'strategic' questions of choice and 'detailed' matters of implementation or enactment, but we suspect this can only be at best part of the story. Moreover, our discussion of the character of the work of middle-ranking officials suggests that this distinction is difficult to sustain in practice as settling 'details' can simultaneously require settling broader strategic or cross-cutting issues.

Our study suggests that middle-ranking officials have characteristics as a group that at first sight make them distinctive players in networks or communities in which they participate. They are likely to be members of this community or network for only a short time and they are unlikely to enter such communities as technical 'experts'. Middle-ranking officials are likely to enter any community or network because of the job they have been assigned rather than any ideological commitment or passion; moreover, the senior officials who judge their performance will not necessarily judge them by their substantive contribution to the policy area but also by how well they handle the process of consulting with those interested and affected by the policy. Procedural success—ensuring that consultation generates no bitterness or helps engineer no defeats or embarrassment—is thus likely to be a more important goal for middle-ranking officials than group members, who might be expected to value more highly success in achieving substantive policy objectives. Most importantly, policy bureaucrats are best considered as delegates when they participate in such networks, whether these networks are national or, through the EU, transnational. They either know or must find out the limits within which their organization will allow them to work and have to ensure that they have some form of clearance or approval before any commitment can be offered. In Gouldner's terms (1957), members or such communities are often assumed to be 'cosmopolitans', whether policy bureaucrats or group members, who look to people outside their own organization for cues about how they should behave, yet middle-ranking officials also have to be 'locals' embedded in some way within the hierarchical structure of their employing organization.

The concentration on middle-ranking bureaucrats as delegates raises the issue of the impact of hierarchies on the operation of networks: how much discretion do members of networks have, how are the constraints within which they operate developed and communicated to them, what motivates members to keep within these boundaries, and do they feel they have the capacity under some circumstances to alter or ignore such constraints? This hierarchical dimension applies not only to bureaucrats; interest group officials are also members of organizations, often employees subject to hierarchical authority and people who pursue lobbying and interest group representation as a career in much the same way as policy officials. To point this out is not to suggest an entirely new dimension to the literature: the discretion of actors features as one variable defining the character of networks and communities (Rhodes 1997). It is rather to highlight its importance since empirical studies tend to concentrate on the relationships within the community rather than those between members and outsiders.

By framing the question of the role of policy bureaucracy in the context of classical bureaucracy theory, we made a decision not to follow current theoretical fashions by framing the question as one of networks or of relations between principals and agents. Perhaps the most important underlying reason for not choosing such approaches, however, remains that if one accepts such theories as network analysis or principal–agent theory as sending sharp shafts of light into public bureaucracies, they illuminate relatively limited aspects of the overall work of policy bureaucrats. Classical bureaucracy theory offers the possibility of a broader understanding of their role without any significant loss of theoretical or methodological rigour.

## The consequences of the trade-off between hierarchy and expertise

We should not be surprised that for much of the time the pattern of dealing with the tension between hierarchy and technical expertise suggested by the ideas of improvised expertise and invited or demand-led authority produces little evidence of dysfunction. While we are not claiming that such patterns of improvised expertise and invited authority were consciously adopted as a response to combat this tension, we are claiming that such norms have developed within the UK civil service and that they provide a way in which a degree of technical expertise can be mobilized in the service of political objectives. Since they serve this function it is possible they serve it in a manner that generally avoids conflict or the frustration of politicians' objectives and allows a sufficient degree of technical expertise to be brought into the policy process. Crozier's *Bureaucratic Phenomenon* (1964) offers the insight that bureaucratic traits—in France the 'horror of face-to-face relationships' among workers in bureaucratic organizations and their reliance on formal mechanisms of authority to govern relation-ships between different levels—serve to allow individuals to man-age hierarchical relationships and retain their own individuality in an organization.

It does not necessarily follow that such bureaucratic traits in-variably produce pathologies in the way Crozier assumes they will, and it is possible to argue that his criticism of the French politico-administrative system does not follow through the impli-cations of the functional logic on which he builds his analysis. For Crozier (1964, 1971) the blockages in the bureaucracy created by the poor flow of information between levels and the total reliance on formal mechanisms of authority to get anything done produce a 'stalled society'. The remarkable changes in French society since the early 1960s—reforms in education, agriculture, administrative organization, health, transport and roads, and budgeting, to name a few—suggest that such cultural patterns of bureaucracy do not necessarily create insuperable barriers to reform. A consid-erable volume of work done under the auspices of Crozier's *Centre de Sociologie des Organisations* (see Crozier et al. 1974) highlights strategies that political elites have used to overcome the limits of the French bureaucratic system. Of particular importance is the development of groups that constitute 'exceptions' to bureau-cratic rigidities with which elites form strategic alliances to push forward change (a form of cooptation strategy—discussed later). Such 'exceptional' groups have included under the Fifth Republic local 'notables' (Worms 1966), young bureaucrats with moderniz-ing ambitions (Thoenig 1973; Grémion 1979), and compliant trades unions (Keeler 1987; see Bezès and Le Lidec, forthcoming 2005 for a general discussion).

A set of bureaucratic traits around the trade-off between hier-archy and expertise of the kind elaborated by Crozier, and also put forward here, may *apparently* work perfectly well under most cir-cumstances because overt conflict and other problems, such as low worker morale, are avoided. To identify dysfunctions re-quired, for Crozier, setting up some normative external criteria for evaluating how the system should be performing in rather general (a 'better management of human resources') and also rather negative terms (little more specific than that we do not want a 'stalled' society or that the *grands corps* at the top of the civil service have the power to innovate and reform but do not use it) rather than suggesting any particular glaring mistakes. Subsequent analyses by collaborators in the *Centre de Sociologie des Organisations* found some specific instances of suboptimal policy-making including misallocation of capital funds for local government and the hindrance of a national system of highways (Thoenig 1973, Crozier and Thoenig 1975—moreover in both these examples the dysfunctions were primarily produced by the 'exceptions' to the bureaucratic rule rather than by the bureaucratic rule itself). Even so, given the influence of Crozierian theory and the scale of the research effort devoted to it following the *Bureaucratic Phenomenon*, these specific and documentable dysfunctions seem rather sparse.

If we apply this discussion to our findings, it is by no means easy to elaborate the consequences of the patterns of relationships within the Whitehall policy bureaucracy. It is possible that the UK civil service is, in the oft-used cliché, a 'Rolls-Royce'[27] service, although we might change the focus of the metaphor from the power of the engine to the silent efficiency of the luxury car—capable of taking ministers effortlessly where they want to go with little noise from the engine ever reaching them in the back seat where they rest in comfort. Where there is little conflict, there is little likelihood of shortcomings in this relationship surfacing except when a large and glaring error emerges, such as through the major public health scare of BSE after the late 1980s, or when an investigatory body such as the National Audit Office initiates studies into less eye-catching failings. Our examination of the consequences of invited authority and improvised expertise therefore mixes both discussion of known deficiencies documented in studies of major problems and exploration of why these patterns might be expected to produce suboptimal policy.

### Demand-led authority

Since the exercise of hierarchical authority in significant cases tends to be requested by the subordinate and is not generally part of the everyday activity of the superior (whether a politician or senior official), the definition of what needs to be considered by the politician can rest in part with the subordinate. We say 'in part' because there are formal rules about what needs ministerial approval—statutory rules, such as some regulations and other legal or quasi-legal documents that need to be signed by the minister, as well as norms that certain types of issues, such as decisions about the form a public consultation should take, need to be cleared with the minister before action can be taken. The general practice of leaving middle-ranking officials to point out the options and risks and to ask for ministerial decision assumes a level of knowledge and understanding about what is at stake and what could go wrong which is especially hazardous since officials often have no real long-term expertise in the topic concerned.

The case of one official's job in reviewing the progress of the team on the task of restructuring grants to local authorities underlines this aspect of middle-ranking officials' job in identifying things that could go wrong before they are put to the minister (the quote is from a high-flyer working as a Grade 7):

We have been reviewing how we distribute the grant to local authorities. My task in this has been (*a*) the coordination of the reviews being done by the others and (*b*) looking at the policy and presentation of policy and media briefing of ministers and providing some non-specialist, ignorant input into solving technical problems. . . . [It] was about telling technical people the political consequences of what they were coming up with— 'that might be technically right but it is bonkers, you can't do that unless you put something else in too to ameliorate the problem you're creating'.

Thus a policy proposal may, taking a wider view, be 'bonkers', risky, or inept, but not recognized as such by officials dealing with the issue. In such cases the notion that approval by a minister is solicited by those developing the proposal reduces the likelihood that it will be challenged before it has been acted upon.

Several major government blunders have in recent years involved the apparent failure of officials to flag up major issues for ministerial action or decision. Ministerial claims that 'junior officials' did not inform them of something important have proved to be a popular first line of defence for ministers who have subsequently had to accept a larger share of the blame. Yet such problems may also be consequences of the invited authority approach. Bringing an issue to a minister's attention does not guarantee that it will be given serious consideration, but the invited authority pattern places a large burden on officials and exposes ministers to substantial risk. It requires extraordinary foresight for an official to identify today's routine technical detail as the crucial political issue of tomorrow. For example, the issue of the disposal of animal waste moved from being a boring, if not comical, matter of detail to the centre of public health policy in the wake of the BSE scandal of the 1990s (Page 2001: 37).

This drawback of demand-led authority was referred to in the Phillips Inquiry into the BSE outbreak in the late 1980s where middle-ranking civil servants' failure to bring issues to the attention of ministers might have delayed the development of a response to the problem:

It seemed to us that clearer expectations about reporting to top management and to Ministers would have assisted in the handling of BSE and medicines. By way of example, had Ministers been asked explicitly to consider whether existing stocks of vaccines should continue to be used while guaranteed 'clean' replacements were procured, we believe they would have taken a keen interest in the follow-up. This in turn might have influenced the subsequent pace of events and perhaps led to the doubtful material being phased out rather more quickly than in fact happened.    (Phillips 2000: para 1232)

A similar drawback can be seen in the 'fridge mountain' fiasco when the UK government had agreed to an EU regulation setting exacting procedures for the safe disposal of refrigerators. Specialist waste disposal firms were unable to meet the likely demand created by the regulation with the result that old refrigerators were stockpiled in makeshift dumps and there was an increase in fly-dumping. The Select Committee on Environment, Food, and Rural Affairs (2002: para 41) argued:

Mr Meacher [the Minister of State responsible] asserted that 'I do not believe that British civil servants behaved in a deficient or improper way at all, not at all. I have looked at this with great care and do not believe that any person on the British side has failed to do what was necessary in the circumstances'.... Nevertheless, we find it extraordinary that the Minister was unaware that there was a potential problem until July 2001, and that his officials had sought clarification of the Regulation on nine occasions without referring the matter to him.... The fact is that doubts were expressed and queries raised for some months before the Regulation was adopted. All that had to be done was for officials to alert Ministers to the problem, and ensure that the Regulation was not agreed until there was a clear shared understanding of what it meant.

In a third case of defective reporting upwards, the Select Committee on the Treasury looked into revenue collection by HM Customs and Excise (2001: para. 13):

Significant revenue losses began to build up as a result of the conduct of excise fraud investigations from 1994. Ministers of the previous Administration do not appear to have been informed. Customs and Excise had identified these problems by 1998. Yet it was not until June 2000 that Ministers of the present Administration were informed. By then, losses had mounted to several hundred million pounds. We commend Ministers for commissioning the Rocques inquiry. But there can be no excuses for either losses on this scale or for failure to report them to Ministers.

Moreover, failure to report problems to ministers has featured in several reports on how private sector contracts have been managed (Public Accounts Committee 2000).

A second major problem is of accountability arising from  *deemed ministerial approval*. It can be hard to discern at what stage a minister makes a choice—consent can even be oral and it is not necessarily clear precisely what a minister has agreed to. One spectacular example of this problem of deemed ministerial approval can be found in decisions about the ill-fated Scottish

Parliament Building. The Scottish Office before devolution appears to have believed or suggested that ministerial approval had been given for this project, yet no record could be found, and the death of the Secretary of State meant he was unable to clear up the matter of what was approved. *The Scotsman* ('Dewar didn't agree to Holyrood contract', 11 June 2004) published a report on the Fraser Inquiry into the fiasco:

[A former special adviser to the Secretary of State and later First Minister Donald Dewar] said: 'If, as some would argue, this was the biggest single error, it is astonishing the record is silent and that no ministerial sign off occurred.' The first mention of the decision in any official documents is in a minute of a design team meeting on 21 July 1998, which said 'it was agreed by all parties that the Scottish Office should follow the construction management process'. . . . Now the Executive has written to Lord Fraser, acknowledging the lack of ministerial approval for the choice. . . . Civil servant Thea Teale, from the Executive's Holyrood evidence unit, said: 'I can confirm that, having looked through the papers on this subject once again, I can find no record of a note to ministers asking them to sign off in writing the design team's decision.'

Another example of imprecision about whether departmental action was approved by ministers can be found in the episode that led to the Home Office minister Beverley Hughes' resignation in 2004, when a departmental memorandum stated that she had approved procedures to 'fast track' East European migrants to Britain ('Memo traps migrant row minister', *Sunday Times* 28 March 2004).

The difficulty of establishing what a minister did or did not approve comes up in the Treasury Select Committee's inquiry into the Equitable Life collapse when one of the Financial Services Authority's Senior Executives was pressed to tell what kind of ministerial involvement there had been in the regulation of the industry:

*Mr Cousins MP*: Mr Allen's letter of 5 November 1998, to which reference has already been made, refers to 'seeking ministerial approval for a letter'. Of course we know that letter was sent and therefore ministerial approval

was given; was there any other involvement with ministers on this particular issue prior to that point in November 1998?

*Mr Roberts* (FSA): I think that really must be a question you should put to
ministers, not to me.

*Mr Cousins*: The Committee here, of course, is in a little difficulty, as you
will see, because, Mr Roberts, as you will accept, you are one of the very
few points of continuity in the changes of administration of regulation.
(Select Committee on the Treasury 2001: paras 245–6)

It can be difficult to discern precisely to what ministerial approval
has been given. It may even be assumed that ministerial
approval must have been given because something that requires
such approval would not have been done without it.

## *The drawback of improvised expertise*

The potential conflict between hierarchy and expertise is neutral-
ized when the 'experts' are not subject specialists but people with
sets of transferable skills—transferable between different sectors and
even types of jobs. These skills include the ability to identify and
recognize the political and administrative cues from which they
should work, the ability to consult, and the ability to locate and
mobilize sources of expertise. Such officials do not generally have a
very long experience of the specific policy terrain, although they
may well have worked on related issues. Either way they can pick up
experience of sorts quickly before they move on to the next job.

   This improvised expertise removes a sense of proprietorship
that helps underpin the technical 'expert's' claim, or possibly
will, to exercise power or be particularly insistent on one way of
approaching a policy problem as opposed to another. Officials
with such improvised expertise do not have time to develop any
strong feelings about the policy issue or the people, such as interest groups, with whom they interact. This improvised expertise
poses problems for the quality of the technical advice that ministers can expect. Under some circumstances it is possible that an
official can master a policy area in a very short time, but it is

unlikely to be possible all the time. This has implications not only for the quality of the technical advice a minister receives but also for the trust that may be placed in it. It is likely to be very hard for a minister to determine whether the advice he or she is receiving is a submission drafted by someone who has only been in the job a couple of weeks, or whether it is one of the rarer submissions by someone who has been working in the field for years.

The lack of subject expertise has long been diagnosed as a problem of the UK civil service. This criticism was a central point of the Fulton Committee (1968) and can be found in the comparison of the DTI and the German Economics Ministry by Hood et al. (2002: 13), although, as they point out, for economic policy 'it is increasingly unrealistic to expect all the subject expertise needed for effective policy...to be available in-house'. The lack of subject expertise within the civil service is discussed by the National Audit Office inquiry into Regulatory Impact Assessments (RIAs), which pointed to the need for more guidance because of the 'fairly rapid movement of staff within the Civil Service' and the inevitability that 'many policymakers preparing RIAs have little previous experience of RIAs' (National Audit Office 2001*b*: para 20). Lack of familiarity with the subject featured in the Select Committee on Environment, Food, and Rural Affairs' inquiry (2002: paras 41–2) into fridge mountains:

We find it deeply disturbing that the Government signed up to the Regulation whilst still suffering from 'knowledge gaps' about its full impact....Whilst the European Commission must accept some blame for lack of clarity, the overwhelming responsibility for mishandling the implementation of Regulation 2037/2000 lies with the Government. Government officials initially made a judgement that insulating foam within fridges fell under Article 16(3) not Article 16(2); they then argued about the semantics of the phrase 'if practicable' when in fact the practicality of dealing with the foam was abundantly demonstrated by practice in other European countries; they were unaware of the implications of Article 11 for exports of fridges from the UK, and therefore for 'take-back' schemes; despite requesting clarification on so many occasions they failed to resolve the issue; they apparently ignored or reacted very slowly to a host of warnings from interested parties; and despite those warnings and legal advice suggesting that the Regulation would be taken to apply to foam insulation they failed to put in place contingency plans to cope with the problem. This debacle will cost the UK around £40 million, a cost which would not otherwise have been incurred.

One of the general problems with assessing the impact of patterns of improvised expertise and demand-led authority is that, as Hood et al. (2002: 30) note, there is little capacity in government to evaluate 'quality' of policy. Highlighting obvious and public shortcomings as exposed through major scandals and blunders cannot address this. They add:

Not all policy geese can be swans and professionals need to have standards that enable them to distinguish good from bad and better from worse work. Indeed that could be considered as one of the defining features of any profession. Evidently such evaluations are hard to make, given the often hyperpolitical context in which policymaking civil servants work . . . the idea of policy quality audits within Whitehall . . . has been dismissed before in the UK on the grounds of its political sensitivity. . . . Nevertheless [assessing performance] without any capacity to judge the substantive quality of what is produced seems to be a case of Hamlet without the Prince of Denmark. . . . Most of the existing forms of policy assessment have an inherent negativity bias, for instance in audit office reports or particular inquiries that highlight dramatic shortcomings in policy quality. Such inquiries also do not permit an assessment of the substantive quality of civil servants' policy work in the light of the constraints in which they operate.

The selection of problems arising from improvised expertise and invited authority should not be taken as evidence that they are undesirable features of the UK civil service. One can point out their dysfunctional characteristics, but these must be weighed up against the fact that they solve a profound difficulty: addressing the conflict between hierarchy and expertise found in all bureaucracies.

## Policy officials as 'representative' bureaucrats

We have presented a picture of a distinctive UK approach to policy bureaucracy, but are its main features to be found in any bureaucracy, public or private, and in any country? The broad features of our characterization of UK policy bureaucracy are that policy officials at relatively junior levels are given substantial responsibility for developing and maintaining policy and servicing other, formally superior officials or bodies, often by offering influential advice and guidance. These people are not technical specialists in the sense that they develop high levels of technical expertise in one subject or stay in the same job for a long time. They are often left with apparently substantial discretion to develop policy because they often receive vague instructions about how to do their jobs, are not closely supervised, and work in an environment that is in most cases not overtly hierarchical. They nevertheless make every effort to gain the technical expertise needed for policy work and to accommodate the minister— they use every cue they can find to produce policies that are what he or she wants or can be expected to want. *Their specialization thus rests primarily in knowing how policy is made and acquiring sufficient technical knowledge to help make it.* Officials will at key stages seek direct approval from ministers who will be given the chance to approve or veto the lines of policy development their civil servants pursue. Direct ministerial approval is required to authorize departmental decisions once policies have been developed, whether they are implemented by primary legislation, secondary regulations, advisory circulars, codes of guidance, or other types of instrument.

Several features of this picture correspond to those of bureaucratic organizations and are not unique to the UK policy bureaucracy. The idea that specialized work (albeit in the case of the UK civil service based on improvised expertise) is done lower down in an organization, and that senior levels tend not to specialize in particular subjects, is a common feature of public and private organizations. Gouldner (1954: 225–6) argues that in the gypsum mine the 'expert...never wins the complete trust of his company's highest authorities and tends to be kept at arm's length from the vaults of power'. He added that 'possibly' the 'most familiar of all' features of his gypsum mine study was the commonplace separation between 'line' and 'staff' authorities with the usual subordination of the latter.... '[S]taff' authority was defined as 'consultative'; staff people could *advise* but they could not *command*.... [They were] divested of 'imperative control'. And normally an organization's experts are located in its staff system.

Moreover, the career expectations of specialists in Gouldner's study are close to those of UK policy civil servants, since the expert was, in the gypsum mine, 'under constant pressure to forego the active pursuit of his specialty if he wished to make headway in the Company hierarchy'. He cites the top company executive with an engineering Ph.D. who 'never mentioned it or gave any indication of it whatsoever, and apparently preferred that it be forgotten' (Gouldner 1954: 226).

The informality of the organizational structure in which policy bureaucrats work might also be expected to be if not universal at least widespread. Gouldner's work offers some reasons for thinking that such informality is a more general feature of organizations like policy bureaucracies. Gouldner makes the distinction between a 'punishment-centred bureaucracy' in which rules and hierarchies play a large part in everyday behaviour and a 'representative bureaucracy' in which the role of formal rules and hierarchy are less pronounced.

First, Gouldner (1954: 221–2) argues that representative bureaucracies are more likely to be found where there is skill specialization, which acknowledges that people formally lower down in the hierarchy have a legitimate claim to an authoritative voice. In the UK policy bureaucracy officials are not technical experts in a traditional sense of having training or long experience in a relatively narrow area, but rather in the sense that they are people having the time to devote to technical issues even if they are not formally trained in them. Second, Gouldner argues that representative bureaucracy and flatter hierarchies are more likely to be found where there is likely to be resistance to formal rules because of the nature of the job—Gouldner's gypsum miners stressed the danger the miners faced daily:

An analogy between men working at the face of a mine and soldiers at the front line is perhaps not too far fetched. Every soldier who has experienced battle conditions is aware that officers at the front behave quite differently than they do in the training camps. When those in authority share a dangerous situation with their subordinates, rigid and formal relationships are greatly diminished.    (Gouldner 1954: 153)

Death through the collapse of a mineshaft is not something that civil servants face, and they are not facing an enemy intent on killing them. The idea that 'we have to do things fast' and to an unpredictable political timetable could, however, have the same hierarchy-flattening consequences. Changed political strategies can mean rewriting policy in short order, or the sudden glare of media attention can generate ministerial requests for a flurry of briefings and papers bringing close and frequent contact with the minister. Third, representative bureaucracy requires some consensus on values and ends (Gouldner 1954: 224), since formal/hierarchical methods of seeking compliance are more likely to be needed 'when subordinates are ordered to do things divergent from their own ends'. We cannot say that the officials we spoke to in the UK civil service personally agree with the policy initiatives or directions they are working on. Yet officials serve ministers and accept that ministers' instructions legitimately override whatever objections they may raise or harbour. Thus there is unlikely to be significant divergence between the values and ends of officials and their political superiors in the development of policy.

The UK policy bureaucracy has the character of a representative bureaucracy, and Gouldner's theory helps us understand why it should be so. In predictions about behaviour in such organizations, Gouldner's approach (1954: 216–17) tackles the treatment of poor performance or deviance. Unlike a punishment-centred bureaucracy, where deviance from accepted rules is seen as voluntaristic and wilful, in representative bureaucracies 'deviance is attributed to ignorance or well-intentioned carelessness—i.e. it is an unanticipated by-product of behaviour oriented to some other end and thus an "accident". This we call a "utilitarian" conception of deviance'. This observation is certainly borne out by the officials we spoke to. On several occasions we asked officials what happened when they got things wrong, and none of the responses indicated they attracted any individual blame. A typical reaction came from an HEO who had written some regulations:

[T]he regs had to specify postcodes so that people in the postcodes covered could get their benefits. Here we were dependent on the people in the field giving us the codes as they are the only ones who would know them. Some were wrong. It became a big issue. Ones that were in the scheme but not in the list did not get their benefit. That became an accounting officer/permanent secretary issue and we had to do a submission to the Secretary of State. And we had to come up with a solution. There was no harm done. We did not get the blame for that. We had to write the submission, which we could do in a way that avoided blaming ourselves. In fact the postcodes had been incorrect . . . [all along before we had them passed on to us]. You cannot imagine what a terrible job it is proofing so many hundreds of postcodes.

A 'blame culture' in policy bureaucracy probably only becomes apparent once mistakes reach public attention, otherwise mistakes appear to attract no individual censure. The idea that the type of work conducted by policy officials tends to create bureaucracies in which hierarchy is less important is also suggested by Damaška (1986) in his analysis of judicial organization. Damaška argues that there are two 'ideals' of officialdom: hierarchical and coordinate. The hierarchical is the one with which we are familiar from Weber's characterization (1988) of bureaucracy since it is 'characterized by a professional corps of officials organized into a hierarchy which makes decisions according to technical standards' (Damaška 1986: 17). The coordinate ideal is 'defined by a body of non-professional decision-makers, organized into a single level of authority which makes decisions by applying undifferentiated community standards' (Damaška 1986: 17). In any system, even one that otherwise manifests strong features of hierarchical ideals of officialdom, political decision-making by its nature—applying undifferentiated community standards—is more likely to reflect a coordinate ideal. Indeed, many of the apparently distinctive features of the EU administrative system, its internal administrative structure, the fact that observers are struck by the role that officials below the top ranks play in policymaking, and the informality of policy processes, may be explained by the proposition that the EU is primarily a policy bureaucracy, while many national bureaucracies combine policy with service provision functions (see Page 1997).

## Representative bureaucracy and its alternatives

Although Gouldner's discussion of representative bureaucracy gives us good theoretical reasons for believing that the work of policy bureaucracies challenges hierarchical authority, there is something distinctly cultural about the UK approach to handling the conflict between authority and expertise in much the same way as Crozier's discussion (1964) of 'bureaucracy as a cultural phenomenon' explained attitudes to authority and their consequential bureaucratic patterns of behaviour as the product of deeper-rooted French cultural attitudes to power and the state. The UK approach to dealing with the conflict—according to which both expertise and hierarchy are suppressed—corresponds to a general and well-known UK pattern of minister–civil servant relations, even though characterizations of these relations are generally based on an understanding of the role of senior civil servants. The ability of the permanent secretary to anticipate the wishes of the politician is part of the central joke in the television and radio comedy programme *Yes, Minister* (Lynn and Jay 1981), which is acclaimed by politicians and civil servants alike as offering a clearly recognizable account of the way that Whitehall works (even though it now features more heavily in official accounts as a representation of all that was wrong with the civil service and a main target of government reform of the civil service and civil service practices—see, e.g. Wilson 2001). The idea that the Whitehall official knows what the politician wants before the politician knows it has strong echoes of the relationship between the gentleman and his manservant in P. G. Wodehouse's Jeeves stories (Wodehouse 1923). We may add to this the charge associated with the Fulton Committee Report (1968) that the civil service is based on the 'cult of the generalist' and the amateur (critically examined in Kellner and Crowther-Hunt 1980:  29–30, see also footnote 19 for a discussion of the applicability of the term 'amateur'), a charge expressed far more positively in descriptions of good 'non-specialist' civil servants as having 'fine analytical minds, [capable of] lucid exposition of issues in writing and the ability to discuss matters with clarity and conviction before Ministers' (Cabinet Office 2004c: 21).

## Representative bureaucracy in the USA

The form of representative bureaucracy we have described in the UK policy bureaucracy is one possible way of dealing with the conflict between hierarchy and expertise. We can call it a *norm-based* approach to the issue because it is based not on any special organizational mechanisms, but on sets of understandings and routines within an ostensibly monocratic organizational structure: the minister at the top, the grades running from the most senior permanent secretary down through the middle ranks to the executive and administrative officers below them. While the existence of special advisers and other bodies might be expected to cloud this clear hierarchy, they do not do so sufficiently strongly and consistently to alter the basic pattern. The UK pattern is unlikely to be the only norm-based representative form of policy bureaucracy.

It might first appear curious to talk of a US policy bureaucracy since our starting definition of the term seems to be predicated on a ministerial administrative structure of the European form. In Europe policy bureaucracies are part of a centralized bureaucracy in a system of party government where the legislature or any other groups have little direct power over the executive. Top political leaders can ask bureaucrats to prepare policies which they know can be put on the statute books more or less as they have been drafted within the executive. In the USA the staffs of agencies (*a*) do not have the confidence of UK civil servants that what they recommend to their political superior within the agency, to political executives, will be, if accepted just by the political executive, part of the legislation passed by Congress; (*b*) have several 'political masters' including different agencies of federal executive (such as the Office of Management and Budget (OMB)) as well as diverse legislative committees and subcommittees that might be interested in any policies they are working on; and (*c*) will be in competition for influence with their diverse political superiors with other groups—lobbies, Congressional staffers, other parts of the executive.

In the USA, policy bureaucracies—officials whose job it is to help write legislation—are found in the legislative as well as the executive branch: within the executive agencies and in the staffs of congressional committees. Moreover, legislation is also written by individuals and groups outside government. The US public policy literature is very thin on this aspect of its bureaucracy and thus our suggestions can only be rather tentative. Within the legislative branch can be found staffers at both the federal and state level who have enough familiarity and expertise with policy issues to do detailed policy work of the kind done by the executive civil servants in the UK. In some cases Congressional staffers appear to have greater expertise than agency officials. The interest and participation of agencies varies according to the issue at hand, the balance of political forces as well as the strength of executive and Congressional leadership. Of the great amount of legislation passed as part of appropriations acts and as amendments to existing major laws each year, the leadership and legislative office of an agency drafts legislation and seeks OMB legislative clearance for the proposals. But this seems to be quite variable. A Congressional insider wrote (in private correspondence):

The size of the staffs of committees, members, and support agencies is impressive and provides virtually complete information on any topic and issue. Thus, very few issues drop in from the outside cold. The management detail questions, one would think, would be developed downtown, through OMB and then the committees would debate these proposals. But my experience is that even the details are just as likely to be developed and promoted here with the executive agencies being in the position of responding to Congressional initiatives.

Thus to find out about policy bureaucracies one needs to look at Congress and legislative staffers as well. In addition, the bureaucracies outside of government in interest groups, professional organizations, and non-profit organizations such as think tanks are larger than in most of Europe and have the capacity to shape legislation through the legislative branch not available to their European counterparts.

The consequence of this pattern of policy bureaucracy in the USA is that the role of the policy bureaucrat certainly *within the executive* and possibly also within the legislative branch has a much greater emphasis on *lobbying* and *advocating* than civil servants doing policy work in the UK, or probably Europe more generally, where the emphasis is on *designing*. Agency policy can be developed without the kind of close legislative approval where there is the scope for issuing administrative regulations. Although the provisions of the Federal Administrative Procedure Act of 1946 still offer some substantial room for legislative involvement (see Kerwin 1999), this often gives significant discretion to agencies, especially in the many cases where Congressional primary legislation is generally argued to be rather vague—for example, in the case of the Environmental Protection Agency (Hoornbeek 2004).

The Congressional liaison sections of agencies and departments are primarily concerned with feeding information into a wider policy process—Congressional hearings, briefings, and the like—and participating in bills that do not necessarily originate in the agency or department and which the departments might not support. This role of officials in Congressional liaison raises some interesting additional questions about the constraints on bureaucrats about which little is known. At the level of the *states*, or one particular state, we get some insight into some of the dilemmas that bargaining with the legislature brings. Ashworth (2001: 148–9), who served as Texas Commissioner of Higher Education, writes:

My deputy and my legislative liaison cannot check back with me when a committee chair or a legislator is negotiating a deal for us or they have to give a quick response to a proposed accommodation that the politicians are ready to action. . . . It is through the consultations and sharing of thinking and ideas that individuals become prepared for those occasions when they cannot check back with you or with others, when they have to make an independent decision. The more sharing, discussing, and melding of ideas toward a common agency goal, the better chance you have that those independent decisions will be congruent with the agency mission and the long-term plans.

Such problems are undoubtedly exacerbated by the particular problems of the legislative process in Texas, where logjams are common and most bills are settled in a flurry of activity two weeks before the short legislative period ends. However, the more general question remains: How in this rather more diverse and shifting world do bureaucrats know how far they can go? What are the cues that shape their participation in the process? What role does straightforward direction by political or administrative superiors play in the process? You cannot cut your own deal, but need to know an agency or committee or even legislator's position—how are such positions established and how are they communicated or discerned? The questions are somewhat different, but the basic question is the same as that addressed in this book: On what basis can bureaucrats be involved in shaping policy?

The answer is that in the USA, as in other countries, we simply do not know. Delegation has become a fashionable area of study in recent years, but has largely been examined empirically through the design of delegation arrangements (see Thatcher and Stone Sweet 2002) or through the use of proxies (see the use of legislation length in Huber and Shipan 2002) rather than the direct observation of behaviour in policy bureaucracies. From the little we know we would expect subject specialization to be far higher in the US policy bureaucracy as permanent officials tend to stay longer in the same job and are more likely to be appointed on the basis of such subject knowledge (Aberbach et al. 1981: 71, 52). The type of knowledge about what has been done in the past and about what works in the Washington establishment is likely to be greater at the level of the executive bureaucracy (Heclo 1977). One might also expect the level of technical expertise to be rather lumpy in the sense that some areas of policy expertise are far weaker. For a bureaucracy based upon technical expertise there are bound to be gaps (compared with a UK bureaucracy that claims it can improvise expertise in any area), and such gaps are likely to be found in the many places where the Congressional staffers or interest organizations and lobbyists not only have a greater subject knowledge but also where their knowledge is trusted at least as much as that of executive officials by those within the agency as well as politicians outside it.

On the question of the cues bureaucrats should use to shape policy, we have some evidence from recent US research that agency heads—political executives—can make an impact. The work by Wood and Waterman (1991) about political control suggests that differences in regulatory approach coincide with changes in the heads of agencies. The mechanism by which this coincidence works is not entirely clear—whether the new agency head comes in and tells people what to do, agency officials anticipate what the new chief wants, or some other mechanism is at work remains unanswered. The extent of effects of changes in executive leadership is also unknown.

A number of commentators talk of agency culture, goals, or 'bureau ideology' (see Downs 1967: 237–46; Wilson 1989: 90ff.). If one were looking for cues by which policy bureaucrats orient their behaviour, an agency ideology has perhaps a much stronger role in the USA than in the UK—a set of beliefs that constrain bureaucrats as well as the people leading them. It certainly fits with some of the classical studies of US bureaucracy—Kaufman's *Forest Ranger* (1960) and Selznick's *TVA and the Grass Roots* (1949). The argument that these are very old and are likely to have no place in any modern account might be true, but the frequency with which '*agency* goals'

is cited in modern discussions of the characteristics of US bureaucracy (see Meier 1999: 62–5) and the fact that much about the UK
pattern of improvised expertise and authority on demand was
detected by an American scholar J. D. Kingsley in his 1944 book
*Representative Bureaucracy* (and probably existed long before) suggest that age does not necessarily diminish such observations.

## Other approaches to policy bureaucracy

A *norm-based* approach is only one of a variety of approaches to
the conflict between hierarchy and expertise. Some countries
appear to have *organizational approaches* to handling the issue—
special organizational arrangements outside the formal hierarchy
of the ministry that seek to assert political control over ministerial
organization. It is important to stress 'appear' since the existence
of such institutions does not necessarily mean they are important
in developing policies. Apparently important institutions in the
UK, such as the array of different enforcement-style organizations
in the Cabinet Office (including the Delivery Unit, Office of Public
Service Reform, Strategy Unit, and Corporate Services), have far
less impact on the development of policy than one would expect
(see also Page 2003 for a discussion of the rather indirect role of the
Strategy Unit in developing legislation in which it claimed a direct
hand) and they rarely made an appearance in the accounts of the
daily lives of policy officials we spoke to, and the same (as discussed in Chapter 5) applies to special advisers in the UK. Thus,
the picture in the UK might be expected to apply in other countries too: analysis of how such arrangements identified at the top
of public bureaucracies affect policy work below the top levels of
the bureaucracy is virtually unexplored. It is only possible to offer
some examples based on what we know about the upper reaches
of the politico-administrative system.

A *parallel hierarchy* is a form of organizational alternative to a
norm-based approach to dealing with expertise: a group of officials in close contact with political leaders who have the task of
ensuring that what goes on within a policy bureaucracy is what

the politicians want and can provide sufficient explicit guidance to policy bureaucrats. In this arrangement expertise is closely monitored by a separate organization directly answerable to a politician who can exercise a more immediate and direct influence on the expert than is possible through the rather extended chain of command of the ministerial or agency structure. Such is the logic behind the *cabinet* found in many Continental European countries—the minister in France has among his or her closest advisers officials who know their way around the politico-administrative system, can act as the minister's eyes and ears, and have direct ability to issue commands in the minister's name.

Parallel hierarchies can also be government-wide bodies: the German *Bundeskanzleramt* (Müller-Rommel 2000) and the Swedish Prime Minister's Office (Elder and Page 2000) have separate organizational sections that shadow separate ministries. Yet such organizations can act as parallel hierarchies to shape policy bureaucracies only as far as they bypass existing hierarchies by circumventing conventional ministerial hierarchies and establishing direct supervision of those below the top levels in ministries. In the EU (Ross 1995) Jacques Delors managed to push his agenda for change in part through something similar to a parallel hierarchy, yet the group of allies was only partially represented within his *cabinet*. Officials not in the *cabinet* as well as other Commissioners offered a *parallel network* that bypassed existing Commission structures to generate and maintain a momentum for change in key parts of the Commission—an arrangement that was fluid and had no precise organizational structure.

*Expert co-optation* by which technical expertise is integrated into high politics provides another mechanism for handling the potential conflict between hierarchy and expertise in policymaking. In some bureaucracies, such as the Belgian, Italian, and Greek (Brans and Hondeghem 1999; Cassese 1999; Sotiropoulos 1999), civil servants in ministries are rarely consulted as experts, and expertise is drawn from outside the civil service. The precise mechanism for co-optation may vary. Co-opted experts and the ability to shape the work of bureaucracies may be reflected informally in party organization as suggested by the notion of a 'cartel party' (Katz and Mair 1995) and as reflected in the use of party-affiliated academics and other specialists as ministerial advisers, above all in Italy and Greece. Such incorporation of party-based experts may be effected through some forms of *cabinet* systems, such as in the practice of Belgian *cabinets* of federal ministers to recruit from outside the civil service (at least before 2002—see Brans and Steen, forthcoming 2005). Or expert co-optation may be formally recognized through networks of working parties and committees, which are given formal status in high political decision-making, as is the practice in the EU through a range of bodies including COREPER, permanent working groups, advisory and other committees (Buitendijk and van Schendelen 1995), and even the ad hoc groups set up to prepare issues for Council and summit meetings (Wurzel 1996).

The effects of such mechanisms must for the time being remain speculative. There are other institutional and norm-based mechanisms, but since our understanding of the bureaucratic role in policymaking is exclusively based on the role of top leadership, and since we do not know how far characteristics identified in the top leadership penetrate to have a direct bearing on the work of lower levels in the bureaucracy, we stop here and use this material only to illustrate the possible variety of different arrangements for exerting political control over policy bureaucracies.

## The nature of the bureaucratic state

A dominant question in the study of contemporary public policy in Europe is that of how far countries are 'converging' in their structures of government, and to what degree 'Europeanization' is bringing about increasing similarities in the way they are governed (see Hix and Goetz 2000). Self-styled 'institutionalists' have invented a new jargon, including impressive words such as 'isomorphism' and 'mimetism', and claimed that the pressures on governments to adopt policies and institutions from other countries are strong (see DiMaggio and Powell 1983). The implication of the research reported in this book are that national systems of bureaucracy not only have distinctive organizational structures but also characteristic conventions and customs through which one of bureaucracy's central tensions—that posed by hierarchy and expertise—is dealt with. Whether or not we call such conventions and customs 'cultural' depends in part on preference but also on an understanding of how distinctive such patterns are: whether they are shared by other bureaucracies in the same country and whether they are distinctive from the patterns prevailing in others. We have been able to offer only some tentative discussion on this latter point. However, if we are correct that conventions and customs vary cross-nationally, we can expect the persistence of substantial differences in bureaucratic systems, even if institutional forms tend to converge—witness the different functions an apparently similar *cabinet* system performs in Belgium, France, and Italy.

While the approach adopted in his book emphasizes some cross-national differences, it also highlights a common feature of bureaucratic states. It might appear curious to end affirming the importance of the Weberian understanding of bureaucracy. Not only has the Weberian state generally been assumed to have been superseded by a more entrepreneurial 'reinvented' state (Osborne and Gaebler 1992) but also much of what we have described in this book by way of setting out how the Whitehall-based policy bureaucracy functions seems to run counter to Weberian conceptions of bureaucracy. The informal relations and flattened hierarchies in UK policymaking contrast with the apparent 'top-down' model based on the Prussian bureaucracy at the turn of the century. The willingness of UK civil servants to follow the wishes of their political masters, to the extent of seeking to find out what they want and then of acting accordingly, seems to contradict the image of the self-aggrandizing bureaucracy that many take from Weber's analysis (Jacoby 1973).

We do not think these observations would cause Weber much trouble. By the standards of the comparison Weber was interested in—the long march of world history—even the most entrepreneurial forms of reinvented government are more bureaucratic in

Weber's sense than the patrimonial forms of government of the Middle Ages. That bureaucrats are ultimately subordinate to politicians was central to his understanding of the nature of politics and how it can be distinguished from administration. What is more interesting for Weberian theory is the light our findings throw on the nature of bureaucracy as a *system* of rule. While we are used to looking at Weber's approach to bureaucracy to say something about the relative power and resources of *individuals*, institutions, and groups—whether ministers, civil servants, parliament, or parties—his conclusions about bureaucracy were about its potential to create an 'iron cage of bondage' (*Gehäuse der Hörigkeit*), a system in which a series of powerful constraints limited what is perceived to be possible or desirable, so that nobody, whether politician, senior, middle-ranking, or junior official, exercises any effective choice. Such limits are a consequence of the collective nature of decision-making in modern states.

The growing importance of international government suggests, according to Weiler (1999, see also Rogoff 2000), that a form of decision-making is emerging within the EU which is less amenable to democratic control precisely because of this feature of modern bureaucracy. Rather than 'internationalism' usurping democratic decision-making at the local level by reducing the power of member states, 'infranationalism' is 'based on the realization that increasingly large sectors of Community norm creation are done at a meso level of governance. The actors... are middle-range officials of the Community and the Member States in combination with a variety of private and semi-public bodies players' (Weiler 1999: 98–9). It is hardly surprising that policies in the EU often, according to Richardson (1996: 17), seem to come 'from nowhere'. This observation is unlikely to be confined to the national–international interaction in EU decision-making and is likely to be a more common feature of bureaucratic life.

The interchangeability between the terms 'policymaking' and 'decision-making' in the study of political science and public administration tends to suggest that policies reflect conscious choices. However, even in a modern democratic political system it is possible for measures to become sanctioned and legitimized as public policy without public scrutiny or even much debate within the executive. The complexity of policy resulting from the range of detailed issues that have to be settled before a law or any other measure can begin to have effect means that a policy is the work of many hands. These detailed issues are not mere technicalities but at a minimum usually mean the difference between success or failure to meet the objectives originally behind the policy. At a maximum they can mean recasting the intentions themselves. Further, the ways devised to handle these detailed issues, while the responsibility of the minister and subject to veto an amendment by politicians, frequently mean that it is hard, if not impossible, to detect the independent impact of any one individual's choices on the policy, whether official or politician. Making policy is a collaboration between the two parts of the executive. The officials do their best to develop practical measures that will meet what they perceive as their political masters' priorities and intentions. For their part, ministers depend heavily on what their officials suggest.

The notion that the character of the policymaking process makes choice difficult was suggested by Kingsley's study (1944) of the UK civil service. Our findings are somewhat at variance with Kingsley's, not least because we find that Whitehall is, in comparison with how it appeared to Kingsley when he conducted his research in the 1930s, a somewhat less grade-conscious place. The reliance on the written word is less pervasive than it was over seventy years ago, and officials outside the top levels have a larger role in making policy. Yet the thrust of his findings about the respective roles of ministers on the one hand and officials on the other in the complex bureaucratic process involved in creating policy is similar to ours.

A Minister or a Cabinet committee decides that action be taken in respect of a particular problem. The Minister consults his permanent officials as to possible lines of procedure and as to the probable effects of alternative approaches.... [I]n its preliminary stages [such consultation] is likely to be informal: a conversation with the permanent secretary at lunch, or an informal conference with the higher departmental officials. But eventually it will begin to take the form of memoranda. If the problem is one involving technical considerations, there will be memoranda from the technical officers involved. If it affects other Departments, like the Treasury, there will be memoranda from them and an interdepartmental committee may even be set up to work out details. Junior and senior officers will add facts and express opinions as the growing file moves through the departmental hierarchy. In the process, the relevant facts will be brought to light and the accumulated wisdom of the officials will be focused on the problem. The result will usually be a clear recommendation that a particular line be followed; and that recommendation will be heavily buttressed with supporting data. Under such circumstances, only the bravest or the most foolhardy of ministers will undertake to pursue another course. In the normal progress of events, the outlines of policy will have been determined by departmental memoranda.    (Kingsley 1944: 272)

We would add that under some circumstances the minister's decision 'that action be taken in respect of a particular problem' in the first place could also arise from the work of his or her officials.

The potential limitations of a bureaucratic system are the opposite from bureaucrats taking over decision-making from the politicians. Politicians are clearly at the apex of the executive structure. In comparison with the full range of tasks they oversee, ministers can at best take a close interest only in a small proportion of the decisions taken in their name. They are highly dependent upon officials working within the policy bureaucracy who work hard to fashion policies in ways they think their ministers will like. The question is where the discretion and choice are exercised within this system. Middle-ranking officials do not generally see themselves as exercising political choices, or even having much discretion. Ministers in the UK claim with justification that they make decisions and choices in key major policies. Yet there is a large range of activity—including developing the contours of new programmes and setting out how policies, major and minor, will work in practice—in which their involvement is often sporadic and limited. In such cases it may be hard to find *anyone* responsible for making choices, least of all conscious ones.

# Appendix: The Interviews

The interviews were conducted between August 2001 and August 2003. The number of respondents in each department is listed in Table A.1 (additional incidental conversations with around a dozen additional officials, some of them touching on the substance of the research, are not included). The respondents were not a random sample of officials at the relevant grades (i.e. HEO to Grade 7) in each department. There is no central list of employees working at these grades, and certainly none available to an outside researcher, in any of the major departments studied. Moreover, many people in these grades—and we have no idea of how many because the statistics do not exist—do not do 'policy work'. In order to locate potential respondents, each department was approached to find between five and twelve officials from the relevant grades who do 'policy work'. No attempt was made to specify what 'policy work' was in advance of the selection of respondents, although the term is universally used throughout the civil service by officials of all grades to describe a range of jobs (see Chapter 3). The letter requesting interviews, usually sent to the office of the permanent secretary in each department (and sometimes passed on to its personnel office), specified divisions within the department in which interviews were sought. The divisions were selected to prevent the possibility of interviews being bunched around only one aspect of a department's activity.

Despite these efforts there was some bunching. In one department we interviewed what we took to be (there were no figures available specifying numbers in middle grades) a highly disproportionate number of fast streamers. In another we spoke to slightly more union activists than we would have expected to find in a random sample. Yet since we did not select the respondents, we do not know exactly what sorts of biases could have been introduced

TABLE A.1    Number of interviews per department

| | |
|---|---:|
| Department of Trade and Industry*[†] | 24 |
| Department of Health | 18 |
| Home Office | 14 |
| Department for Work and Pensions | 11 |
| Office of the Deputy Prime Minister | 11 |
| Department for Environment, Food and Rural Affairs | 10 |
| HM Treasury | 10 |
| Ministry of Defence | 10 |
| Department for Education and Skills | 8 |
| Department for Culture, Media and Sport | 4 |
| Land Registry | 4 |
| Lord Chancellor's Department | 2 |
| Scottish Executive* | 2 |
| Total | 128 |

*includes one two-person interview (counted as two interviews).
[†]not counting one follow-up interview.

into the selection. We gained the impression, from what a few respondents said to us, that our respondents were to some degree self-selected—they had agreed to talk to us, suggesting that some of their colleagues had not. However, such self-selection is likely in any sample of this kind—the consent of the respondent is the most basic ethical principle of any form of survey research. Nevertheless, by contrast a handful of respondents indicated, in what we believed to be a half-joking way, some degree of compulsion by having been 'volunteered' for the study by, say, the human resources part of their department. Our justification for accepting such potential, yet unknown and unknowable biases was that this way of establishing contact and gaining permission to interview was the only game in town. Giving up the idea of an empirical study of middle-ranking officials, rather than sampling randomly from a non-existent up-to-date list of HEOs, SEOs, Grade 7s, and Grade 6s, was its only feasible alternative.

As part of this project we also examined the work of civil servants, predominantly at the middle grades that serve as the focus for this book, on four bill teams producing four pieces of legislation: The Adoption and Children Act 2002, The Proceeds of Crime Act 2002, the Employment Act 2002, and the Land Registration Act 2002. The findings of this particular part of the research have been published separately (Page 2003). The interviews for this part of the project are also included in Table A.1, and explain the higher number of interviews in the Home Office, the DTI, and the DoH, which were responsible for three of these pieces of legislation. The fourth, the Land Registration Act, led us to our interviews in the Land Registry and the Lord Chancellor's Department, while they were not included in the original plans. Most of the interviews conducted in the bill teams research have been included in this analysis. In the course of this bill team research four officials in Senior Civil Service grades were also interviewed, and they have been excluded from the figures presented in Table A.1 and in the body of the text (primarily Chapters 2 and 3).

The interviews were scheduled to last for 20 minutes. Where respondents had not finished answering the questions within the 20 minutes, they were explicitly asked whether they were willing to extend the interview beyond 20 minutes, and none refused.

The interviews usually started with the interviewer outlining the study and the conditions under which the interview was to be conducted and an indication that there were only two basic questions to be answered: 'what do you do?' and 'how do you come to be in this job?' Respondents were asked about the work they were doing at the moment. Usually they chose to answer this question by giving background about their unit and the particular policy issue they were dealing with. Occasionally this squeezed discussion of what was going on that day into a short space in the interview. Follow-up questions were posed to understand what respondents did and how they went about their work. Respondents were then asked how they came to be in their jobs and about their careers so far, and follow-up questions in this part of the interview probed how they saw their careers developing. These biographical questions were usually asked towards the end of the interview (although some volunteered the information at the beginning) and usually took around one-fifth of the time taken for the whole interview. Respondents had no difficulty in answering these questions and there were no refusals to respond.

The interviews were not recorded electronically. Notes were taken and written up as soon as possible after the interview(s). In practice interviews were written up in the afternoon or early evening of the day they were conducted. The interviews produced 187,000 words in transcript—1,460 words on average for each interview. Additional material (e.g. consultation documents or organograms) was provided by respondents or taken from the web.

Respondents were told that any quotes would be anonymous. A draft of this book was sent to all respondents as well as to the office of the permanent secretary of each department in which interviews were conducted. As part of the agreement, drafts of the book were also sent to the Cabinet Office and the Public and Commercial Services Union.

# Endnotes

1 The Hutton Inquiry looked into the circumstances of the death of David Kelly, whose status as a middle-ranking official assumed some importance in the press and media coverage of the issue. Kelly's status was not straightforward—we came across no similar complexities among the officials we interviewed—but he was a middle-ranking official in the sense that he remained outside the Senior Civil Service (SCS). He had been given merit promotion to Grade 5 (normally considered the first rung of the SCS ladder) in 1992. Yet this merit promotion was in recognition of his professional expertise and he remained outside the SCS. His new status did not entail the exercise of higher management responsibilities associated with an SCS position. Changes after 1992 in the grading system for civil servants that followed the introduction of new decentralized personnel management arrangements meant that his status (as a Career Level 9 with the Defence Science and Technology Laboratory) became closer to a Grade 6 in the old civil service grades, the highest level outside the SCS.

2 See Home Office *Public Protection News*, 1 July 2002 (London Home Office), p. 1. http://www.probation.homeoffice.gov.uk/files/pdf/public_protection_news_issue_1_july_02.pdf. (accessed July 2004).

3 Some countries, such as the Netherlands, have produced far more by way of academic studies of officials below the very top. See van Braam (1957) and van der Meer and Roborgh (1993).

4 Unfortunately no database exists that would allow us to determine which proportion of those serving in the positions we are interested in—the equivalent of Grades 6 and 7, Senior Executive Officers (SEOs) and Higher Executive Officers (HEOs)—are doing 'policy jobs'.

5 This term was first used in a casual comment by LJ Sharpe (Nuffield College, Oxford) over twenty years ago. In American usage 'first floor' is ground level, the term is used here in its UK meaning of one floor up from ground level.

6 The Directorate was disbanded in 2002, but CMPS continues to exist.

7 The tension can also be found in other classic theories of bureaucracy, notably that of Hegel (1967).

8    His third form of bureaucracy, 'mock bureaucracy', is interesting but underdeveloped.

9    Along with consensus over the goals of the organization, see Gouldner (1954: 221).

10   Taken from Hensher, P., 'Secrets of the bowler hat brigade', *The Independent* 28 July 2004.

11   See    http://www.pcs.org.uk/Templates/internal.asp?NodeID=882796 (accessed 11 September 2004).

12   The Grade 6 and 7 level official earns nearly £20,000 less than the SCS official and £15,000 more than the SEO/HEO, who in turn earns something over £6,000 (depending on whether the comparison is between male or female officials) than the Executive Officer (EO) below him or her (see Table FN12). These salaries are medians, refer to 2002 (the latest year available), and are broken down by merged 'responsibility levels', and thus not comparable with salary levels presented in Table 2.1. While there are more women in these middle categories than at the top, the proportion of women in Grade 6 and 7 jobs is half that of the civil service as a whole; in the SEO/HEO levels, the level is only slightly higher than that for Grade 6/7. The under-representation of ethnic minorities mirrors the under-representation of women in these grades, with under half the civil service average found in Grades 6/7. The age difference between officials in each of the categories is relatively small: as one goes down the grade hierarchy, at each step the average age is around three years lower. The average SEO/HEO grade official is in his or her early forties, the Grade 6/7 in his or her mid-forties, and the average SCS official nearly fifty.

The middle grades we are interested in are substantially compartmentalized from the remainder because entry to an HEO position from a lower grade usually follows a process of selection involving attending an assessment centre, as does promotion from HEO or SEO to Grade 7. Entry to the SCS from Grade 7 is, especially for the non-fast streamer, the biggest hurdle to promotion through the ranks; this is followed by the assessment hurdle between HEO/SEO and Grade 7. Whether it reflects these barriers, or whether there are other reasons such as age or job satisfaction, there is the least movement in and out of Grade 6/7 as measured by the annual resignation and entrance rates.

13   Or rather of the 102 for whom sufficient information was available.

TABLE FN12 Demographics of civil servants by grade

| | Disabled (%) | Women (%) | Median male salary (£k) | Median female salary (£k) | Ethnic minority (%) | Average age | Resignation rate (%) | Entrance rate (%) |
|---|---|---|---|---|---|---|---|---|
| SCS | 1.8 | 21.6 | 63.2 | 61.1 | 2.4 | 49.0 | 2.3 | 4.4 |
| Level 6/7 | 2.4 | 27.3 | 41.6 | 39.1 | 2.9 | 46.1 | 0.6 | 3.8 |
| SEO/HEO | 2.5 | 33.8 | 26.3 | 24.1 | 3.7 | 43.6 | 1.9 | 4.2 |
| EO | 3.6 | 52.6 | 19.5 | 18.6 | 6.2 | 40.8 | 2.1 | 4.6 |
| AA | 3.6 | 62.8 | 13.9 | 13.3 | 7.7 | 38.8 | 5.0 | 11.8 |
| Unknown | 0.1 | 25.7 | | | | | | |
| All | 3.2 | 52.7 | 20.3 | 14.8 | 6.0 | 40.7 | 3.6 | 8.1 |

*Source:* Cabinet Office (2003).

14   Assigning any respondent to a group is a function of their career expectations, as expressed in the interview, and an assessment of the realism of these expectations. Since the interviews did not last long enough to explore how realistic any expectations of promotion might be (perhaps any pessimism or resignation might be exaggerated or misplaced), the categories have to be regarded as approximate. However, in many cases the cues to assign an official to any one group were quite obvious; for example, a person in his or her fifties who had been an HEO for a very long time was justifiably resigned to staying at this grade, while an official in his or her twenties who had joined as a fast stream civil servant and already been promoted to Grade 7 would have every expectation of reaching the SCS—barring resignation, enormous bad luck, or a career-threatening mistake.

15   'Careers in the Department for Transport' www.dft.gov.uk/stellent/groups/dft_about/documents/page/dft_about_507599-05.hcsp   (accessed March 2004).

16   This figure comes from the SCS database, Personnel Statistics, Cabinet Office and was supplied on request by the Corporate Development Group within the Cabinet Office. The figure refers to data on 2,793 staff in post at pay band 1 and excludes those for whom information on degree-level qualifications is unavailable.

17   Now one might expect that HM Treasury employs poachers turned gamekeepers to keep an eye on how spending departments work. In fact this was found in only one of the ten Treasury cases. The large number of people from outside the Treasury who had secondments in it is explained by its reputation as a good and interesting place to work. Officials from outside include a Grade 7 from Export Credits Guarantee Department, a Grade 7 who worked in the Foreign Office and the Scottish Office, and another ex-Foreign Office official who explained his move:

I moved from the FO because my wife was fed up with the postings. If you are in the FO you can expect to spend time abroad, and if your wife works in the city and earns more than you she does not want to be sent out to Khartoum. Also it is more interesting working in the Treasury—in the centre of things.

One official explained that the large number of DCMS officials who were either on secondment or had moved from other departments was a consequence of the fact that 'the department was formed ten years ago. So it is not surprising that people have not been here all that long'. Those who had moved to it also described it as an attractive posting. A Grade 7 who had move there noted:

I stayed in the PCA and did quite well, lots of promotion. But it did not have much of a future as I was not getting that much different experience. I could not believe my luck when I applied for and got the DCMS job. It is a sought-after department and I was interested in what it does.

18   See, for example, Andrew Turnbull, Head of the Home Civil Service 'Civil Service Reform Delivery and Values' London: Cabinet Office 24 February 2004; www.civil-service.gov.uk/reform/event.asp (accessed July 2004). The Centre for Management and Policy Studies of the Cabinet Office published a 'route map' for planning a career that would involve entry into the SCS, which included a section on 'career anchors'; see http://routemap.cmps.gov.uk/ (accessed July 2004).

19   Kingsley (1944: 175) continues 'the underlying assumption in the service as well as outside is the natural superiority of the amateur', a description famously echoed by the Fulton Committee (1968): 'The service is still essentially based on the philosophy of the amateur (or "generalist" or "all-rounder").... The ideal administrator is all too often seen as the gifted layman.' Yet to call officials 'amateurs' because they do not have technical specialization is to confuse specialized technical knowledge of a particular topic with professionalism (as this term is the correct alternative to 'amateurism'). As will be seen in Chapters 3 and 4, policy work requires the application of skills acquired by officials about how to help develop and shape policy that an 'amateur' (whether understood as an outsider suddenly parachuted into the job, or someone doing it as unpaid work in his or her spare time) could not be expected to have.

20   A Private Finance Initiative (PFI) is a scheme that involves private finance in public projects, usually through private companies financing and building a capital project, such as a hospital, and leasing it to the public sector. See Allen (2003).

21   See        http://www.scottishlabour.org.uk/liddellspeech2003/?print= friendly &searchword= (accessed July 2004).

22   The term 'Sewel Motion' derives from the 'Sewel Convention' set out by Lord Sewel, one of the government ministers responsible during the parliamentary stages in the passage of the Scotland Act 1998 that

set up a devolved government in Scotland. Under the Act, the UK Parliament retains the authority to legislate in matters devolved to the Scottish Parliament. The Sewel Convention sets out the principle that the UK Parliament will not do so without the express consent of the Scottish Parliament. The consent of the Scottish Parliament is indicated by a Sewel Motion (see Page and Bailey 2002; Sear 2003).

23   Harpum went on to write the book on the new act (see Harpum and Bignell 2002).

24   The term 'adviser' is used for a variety of non-political civil service and other positions. Many policy workers describe themselves as 'policy advisers', and lawyers in the civil service are formally described as 'legal advisers'. 'Advisers' may also be consultants or academics brought in to give technical advice. An MoD official interviewed had, as a middle-ranking civil servant, held a post of 'political adviser' to the UK contingent of a multinational force stationed abroad, but this refers to a person with responsibility for giving advice on political events in the region to military officers.

25   Colin Thain (in private correspondence in June 2004) explains this exceptional influence of Treasury special advisers in this way: '(a) The Treasury team when Gordon Brown came to power was suspicious of the impact of eighteen years of Tory rule on Treasury officials. There was a deliberate policy of crowding out the "official" Treasury. Advisers were the way of insulating Brown and his team and giving them support. For example, the Bank of England decision was taken with no official support until the very end of the process. The official Treasury has subsequently tried to claw back its influence. Gus O'Donnell is an example of a savvy official who made the leap; (b) Ed Balls was … a pivotal figure here as an example of a special adviser who is more than the conventional somewhat tangential, peripheral adviser of the past. He, more than Alastair Campbell or Jonathan Powell, has revolutionized the way such figures are regarded. Of course, his position has now been regularized in true British (and Treasury) tradition by making him Chief Economic Adviser; (c) In the Treasury culture or mode of operation, Special Advisers have never been so disdained in the Treasury as in other departments. Treasury officials want to get into "the mind" of the Minister. A good, capable adviser is an aid to this. In fact the Treasury has institutionalized this as Chief Economic Adviser. A job that was im-

portant under Margaret Thatcher (Terry Burns, then followed by Alan Budd both British monetarists).' Ed Balls resigned in 2004 preparatory to standing as a Labour candidate in the election anicipated for 2005.

26   Ironically the bill managed to generate one of the biggest embarrassments for the Conservative opposition through forcing into the open intraparty conflict over attitudes to homosexuality over the issue of whether same-sex couples should be allowed jointly to adopt children (see Page 2003; 'Tory leader defied over gay adoption' *Daily Telegraph* 5 November 2002).

27   The term comes from Rab Butler: 'The civil service is a bit like a Rolls-Royce. You know it's the best machine in the world, but you're not quite sure what to do with it.'

# Bibliography

Aberbach, J. D., Putnam, R. D., and Rockman, B. A. (1981). *Bureaucrats and Politicians in Western Democracies.* Cambridge, MA: Harvard University Press.

Allen, G. (2003). *The Private Finance Initiative, House of Commons Research Paper 03/79.* London: House of Commons Library, October.

Ashworth, K. (2001). *Caught Between the Dog and the Fireplug, or How to Survive Public Service.* Washington, DC: Georgetown University Press.

Axelrod, R. (1984). *The Evolution of Cooperation.* New York: Basic Books.

Baker, J. (2004). *Twenty-Sixth Annual Report on Senior Salaries* (Cmnd. 6099). London: HMSO.

Barberis, P. (1996). *The Elite of the Elite: Permanent Secretaries in the British Higher Civil Service.* Aldershot: Dartmouth.

Bevir, M. and Rhodes, R. A. W. (2003). *Interpreting British Governance,* London and New York: Routledge.

Bezès, P. and Le Lidec (forthcoming 2005). 'The French Senior Civil Service', in E. C. Page and V. Wright (eds.), *The Senior Bureaucracy in the Service State.* Houndsmill: Palgrave.

Blau, P. (1955). *The Dynamics of Bureaucracy.* Chicago: University of Chicago Press.

Brans, M. and Hondeghem, A. (1999). 'The Senior Civil Service in Belgium', in E. C. Page and V. Wright (eds.), *Bureaucratic Elites in Western European States—A Comparative Analysis of Top Officials.* Oxford: Oxford University Press.

Brans, M. and Steen, T. (forthcoming 2005). 'From Incremental to Copernican Reform? Changes to the Position and Role of Senior Civil Servants in the Belgian Federal Administration', in E. C. Page and V. Wright (eds.), *The Senior Bureaucracy in the service state.* Houndsmill: Palgrave.

Buitendijk, G. J. and Van Schendelen, M. P. C. (1995). 'Brussels Advisory Committees: a Channel for Influence?', *European Law Review,* 20: 37–56.

Cabinet Office (2003). *Civil Service Statistics 2002.* London: HMSO.

—— (2004a). 'Professional Skills for Government: Core Briefing'. London: Cabinet Office, available at http://www.civil-service.gov.uk/reform/documents/Briefingpsg.doc (accessed October 2004).

Cabinet Office (2004*b*). *Civil Service Statistics 2003*. London: HMSO.

—— (2004*c*). *Civil Service Reform Delivery and Values*. London: Cabinet Office, available at http://www.civil-service.gov.uk/reform/documents/delivery_values.pdf (accessed October 2004).

Carpenter, D. P. (2001). *The Forging of Bureaucratic Autonomy: Reputations, Networks, and Policy Innovation in Executive Agencies 1862–1928*. Princeton, NJ: Princeton University Press.

Cassese, S. (1999). 'Italy's Senior Civil Service: An Ossified World', in E. C. Page and V. Wright (eds.), *Bureaucratic Elites in Western European States— A Comparative Analysis of Top Officials*. Oxford: Oxford University Press.

Centre for Management and Policy Studies (CMPS) (2001). *Better Policy Making*. London: CMPS.

Crozier, M. (1964). *The Bureaucratic Phenomenon*. London: Tavistock.

—— (1971). *La société bloquée*. Paris: Seuil.

—— and Thoenig, J-C. (1975). 'La régulation des systèmes organisées complexes', *Revue Française de Sociologie*, 16 (1): 3–32.

Crozier, M., Friedberg, E., Grémion, C., Grémion, P., Thoenig, J-C., and Worms, J-P. (1974). *Où va l'administration française?* Paris: Editions d'organisation.

Damaška, M. R. (1986). *The Faces of Justice and State Authority: A Comparative Approach to the Legal Process*. New Haven, CT: Yale University Press.

Department for Transport (undated *c*. 2003). *Careers in the Department for Transport*. London: Department of Transport, available at http://www.dft.gov.uk/stellent/groups/dft_about/documents/page/dft_about _507599-05.hcsp (accessed January 2004).

DiMaggio, P. and Powell, W. W. (1983). 'The Iron Cage Revisited: Institutional Isomorphism and Collective Rationality in Organizational Fields', *American Sociological Review*, 48: 147–60.

Dowding, K. (1995) *The Civil Service*, London and New York: Routledge.

Downs, A. (1967). *Inside Bureaucracy*. Boston, MA: Little, Brown & Co.

Dunleavy, P. (1991). *Democracy, Bureaucracy and Public Choice: Economic Explanations in Political Science*. London: Harvester.

Elder, N. C. M. and Page, E. C. (2000). 'Sweden: The Quest for Coordination', in B. G. Peters and V. Wright (eds.), *Administering the Summit: Administration of the Core Executive in Developed Countries*. London: Palgrave.

Fulton Committee (1968). *The Civil Service*, Vol. 1, *Report of the Committee 1966–68* (Cmnd. 3638). London: HMSO.

Gay, O. (2004). *The Lyons and Gershon Reviews and Variations in Civil Service Conditions: House of Commons Standard Note SN/PC 2588*. London: House of Commons, March (available at http://www.parliament.uk/commons/lib/research/notes/snpc-02588.pdf (accessed July 2004).

Gershon, P. (2004). *Releasing Resources for the Front Line: Independent Review of Government Efficiency*. London: HMSO for HM Treasury.

Goodsell, C. T. (2004). *The Case for Bureaucracy: A Public Administration Polemic*, 4th edn. Chatham House, NJ: Chatham House.

—— (ed.) (1981). *The Public Encounter: Where State and Citizen Meet*. Bloomington, IN: Indiana University Press.

Gouldner, A. W. (1954). *Patterns of Industrial Bureaucracy*. New York: Free Press.

—— (1957). 'Cosmopolitans and Locals: Toward an Analysis of Latent Social Roles – I', *Administrative Science Quarterly*, 2: 281–306.

—— (1968). 'The Sociologist as Partisan: Sociology and the Welfare State', *American Sociologist*, 3: 103–16.

Gray, A. and Jenkins, W. I. (2003). 'Government and Administration: Paradoxes of Policy Performance', *Parliamentary Affairs*, 56(2): 170–87.

Grémion, C. (1979). *Profession decideurs: Pouvoir des hauts fonctionnaires et reforme de l'etat*. Paris: Gauthier-Villars.

Grémion, P. (1992). 'Michel Crozier's Long March: The Making of *The Bureaucratic Phenomenon*', *Political Studies*, XL(1): 5–20.

Harpum, C. and Bignell, J. (2002). *Registered Land—The New Law: A Guide to the Land Registration Act 2002*. London: Jordans.

Heclo, H. (1977). *A Government of Strangers: Executive Politics in Washington*, Washington: Brookings Institution.

Heclo, H. and Wildavsky, A. B. (1974). *The Private Government of Public Money*. London: Macmillan.

Hegel, G. W. F. (1967). *Hegel's Philosophy of Right* (trans. T. M. Knox). Oxford: Oxford University Press.

Hill, M. and Hupe, P. L. (2002). *Implementing Public Policy*. London: Sage.

Hix, S. and Goetz, K. H. (2000). 'Introduction: European Integration and National Political Systems', *West European Politics*, 23(4): 1–26.

Hofstede, G. (1979). *Culture's Consequences: Comparing Values, Behaviors, Institutions, and Organizations Across Nations*. London: Sage.

Home Office (1998). *Organized and International Crime Directorate Working Group on Confiscation Third Report: Criminal Assets*. London: Home Office.

Hood, C. and Lodge, M. (2004). 'Competency, Bureaucracy and Public Management Reform: A Comparative Analysis', *Governance*, 17(3): 313–34.

Hood, C., Lodge, M., and Clifford, C. (2002). *Civil Service Policy-Making Competencies in the German BMWi and British DTI: A Comparative Analysis Based on Six Case Studies*. London: Smith Institute.

Hooghe, L. (2001). *The European Commission and the Integration of Europe: Images of Governance*. Cambridge: Cambridge University Press.

Hoornbeek, J. A. (2004). Runaway Bureaucracies or Congressional Control? Water Pollution Policies in the American States, Ph.D. dissertation, University of Pittsburgh.

Huber, J. D and Shipan, C. R. (2002). *Deliberate Discretion? The Institutional Foundations of Bureaucratic Autonomy*. Cambridge: Cambridge University Press.

Hutton, Lord (2004). *Report of the Inquiry into the Circumstances Surrounding the Death of Dr David Kelly HC 247*. London: HMSO.

Jacoby, H. (1973). *The Bureaucratization of the World*. Berkeley, CA: University of California Press.

Jordan, A. G. and Richardson, J. J. (1982). 'The British Policy Style or the Logic of Negotiation', in J. J. Richardson (ed.), *Policy Styles in Western Europe*. London: Allen and Unwin.

Kassim, H. and Menon, A. (2002). 'The Principal–Agent Approach and the Study of the European Union: A Provisional Assessment', Birmingham, The European Research Institute Working Paper Series (not numbered), 14 July.

Katz, R. and Mair, P. (1995). 'Changing Models of Party Organisation and Party Democracy: The Emergence of the Catch-All Party', *Party Politics*, 1(1): 5–28.

Kaufman, H. (1960). *The Forest Ranger: A Study in Administrative Behavior*. Baltimore: Johns Hopkins Press.

Kavanagh, D. and Richards, D. (2001). 'Departmentalism and Joined-up Government: Back to the Future?', *Parliamentary Affairs*, 54(1): 1–18.

Keeler, J. (1987). *The Politics of Neocorporatism in France: Farmers, the State and Agricultural Policy-making in the Fifth Republic*. New York and Oxford: Oxford University Press.

Kellner, P. and Crowther-Hunt, Lord (1980). *The Civil Servants: An Inquiry into Britain's Ruling Class*. London: MacDonald and Janes.

Kerwin, C. M. (1999). *Rulemaking: How Government Agencies Write Law and Make Policy*. Washington, DC: Congressional Quarterly Press.

Kelsen, H. (1945). *General Theory of Law and State*. Cambridge, MA: Harvard University Press.

Kiewiet, D. R. and McCubbins, M. D. (1991). *The Logic of Delegation*. Chicago: University of Chicago Press.

Kingdon, J. W. (1985). *Agendas, Alternatives, and Public Policies*. New York: HarperCollins.

Kingsley, J. D. (1944). *Representative Bureaucracy*. Yellow Springs, OH: Antioch Press.

Krause, G. A. and Meier, J. K. (2003). 'The Scientific Study of Bureaucracy: An Overview', in Krause, G. A. and Meier, J. K. (eds.), *Politics, Policy, and Organizations: Frontiers in the Scientific Study of Bureaucracy*. Ann Arbor, MI: University of Michigan Press.

Kuper, H. and Marmot, M. (2003). 'Job Strain, Job Demands, Decision Latitude, and Risk of Coronary Heart Disease within the Whitehall II Study', *Journal of Epidemiology and Community Health*, 57:147–53.

Labour Party (2001). *Ambitions for Britain, Labour's Manifesto 2001*. London: Labour Party.

Law Commission (1998). *Land Registration for the Twenty-First Century. A Consultative Document*. London: Law Commission No 254.

—— (2001). *Land Registration for the Twenty-First Century: A Conveyancing Revolution*. London: Law Commission No 71.

Lipsky, M. (1980). *Street-Level Bureaucracy: The Dilemmas of Individuals in Public Services*. Cambridge, MA: MIT Press.

Lynn, J. and Jay, A. (1981). *Yes Minister: The Diaries of a Cabinet Minister by the Rt Hon. James Hacker MP*. London: BBC.

Meier, K. J. (1999). *Politics and the Bureaucracy: Policymaking in the Fourth Branch of Government, 4th edn*. Belmont, CA: Wadsworth Publishing.

Merton, R. K. (1940). 'Bureaucratic Structure and Personality', *Social Forces*, 18(4): 560–76.

Milgrom, P. and Roberts, J. (1992). *Economics, Organization and Management*. Englewood Cliffs, NJ: Prentice-Hall.

Moe, T. (1984). 'The New Economics of Organization', *American Journal of Political Science*, 28(4): 739–77.

Morris, S., Greenberg, D. R., et al. (2003). *Designing a Demonstration Project: An Employment, Retention and Advancement Demonstration for Great Britain*. London: Cabinet Office Strategy Unit, Government Chief Social Researcher's Office Occasional Paper Series, April.

Müller-Rommel, F. (2000). 'Management of Politics in the German Chancellor's Office', in B. G. Peters and V. Wright (eds.), *Administering the Summit: Administration of the Core Executive in Developed Countries*. London: Palgrave.

National Audit Office (2001*a*). *Joining Up to Improve Public Services* (HC383). London: HMSO.

—— (2001*b*) *Better Regulation Making Good Use of RIAs* (HC329). London: HMSO.

Niskanen, W. A. (1971). *Bureaucracy and Representative Government*. Chicago: Aldine Atherton.

Office for National Statistics (2004). *Regional Trends 38*. London: HMSO.

Office for Public Services Reform (OPSR) (2002). *Identifying Good Practice in the Use of Programme and Project Management in Policy-Making: Practitioners' Perspectives*. London: Office of Public Services Reform.

Osborne, D. and Gaebler, T. (1992). *Reinventing Government: How the Entrepreneurial Spirit is Transforming the Public Sector*. New York: Penguin Books.

Page, A. and Bailey, A. (2002). 'Scotland's Other Parliaments', *Public Law*, Autumn: 501–23.

Page, E. C. (1997). *People Who Run Europe*. Oxford: Oxford University Press.

—— (2001). *Governing by Numbers: Delegated Legislation and Everyday Policy Making*. Oxford: Hart.

—— (2003). 'The Civil Servant as Legislator: Law Making in British Administration', *Public Administration*, 81(4): 651–79.

Parsons, W. (1995). *Public Policy: An Introduction to the Theory and Practice of Policy Analysis*. Cheltenham: Edward Elgar.

Performance and Innovation Unit (2000) *Wiring it Up: Whitehall's Management of Cross-Cutting Policies and Services*. London: HMSO.

Peters, B. G. (2000). *The Politics of Bureaucracy*. London: Routledge.

Phillips, Lord (2000). *Inquiry into the Emergence and Identification of Bovine Spongiform Encephalopathy (BSE) and Variant Creutzfeldt–Jakob Disease (vCJD) and the Action Taken in Response to it up to 20 March 1996* (Chair: Lord Phillips of Worth Matravers), 15 vols. London: HMSO.

Pressman, J. and Wildavsky, A. B. (1973) *Implementation. How Great Expectations in Washington are Dashed in Oakland*. Berkeley, Calif., University of California Press.

Public Accounts Committee (2000). *Twenty-fourth Report. The Passport Delays of Summer 1999* HC 208. London: HMSO.

Pulzer, P. (1967). *Political Representation and Elections in Britain*. London: George Allen and Unwin.

Rhodes, R. A. W. (1997). *Understanding Governance*. Milton, Keynes: Open University Press.

Richards, D. and Smith, M. (2002). *Governance and Public Policy in the UK*. Oxford: Oxford University Press.

Richardson, J. (1996). 'Policy-making in the EU: Interests, Ideas and Garbage Cans of Primeval Soup', in J. Richardson, (ed.), *European Union: Power and Policy-Making*. London and New York: Routledge.

Ridley, F. F. (ed.) (1968). *Specialists and Generalists: A Comparative Study of the Professional Civil Servant at Home and Abroad*. London: George Allen and Unwin.

Rogoff, M. A. (2000). 'European Integration: Past, Present, and Future' *Vanderbilt, Journal of Transnational Law*, 33(5): October, available at http://law.vanderbilt.edu/journal/33-05/33-5-5.htm (accessed July 2004).

Rose, R. (1981). 'The Political Status of Higher Civil Servants in Britain', *Studies in Public Policy* No 92. Glasgow: University of Strathclyde Centre for the Study of Public Policy.

Ross, G. (1995). J*acques Delors and European Integration*. New York and London: Polity Press.

Rouban, L. (1999). 'The Senior Civil Service in France', in E. C. Page, and V. Wright, (eds.), *Bureaucratic Elites in Western European States*. Oxford: Oxford University Press.

Scott, G. (1999). *Controlling the State: Constitutionalism from Ancient Athens to Today*. Cambridge, MA/London: Harvard University Press.

Sear, C. (2003). 'The Sewel Convention', *House of Commons Library Standard Note* 27 February 2003, available at http://www.parliament.uk/commons/lib/research/notes/snpc-02084.pdf (accessed September 2004).

Select Committee on Environment, Food and Rural Affairs (2002). *Fourth Report Disposal of Refrigerators, HC 673*. London: HMSO, June 2002.

Select Committee on Public Administration (2001). *Fourth Report. Special Advisers: Boon or Bane? HC 293*. London: HMSO.

—— (2002). *Eighth Report. These Unfortunate Events: Lessons of Recent Events at the Former DTLR HC 303*. London: HMSO.

Select Committee on the Treasury (2001a). *Equitable Life and the Life Assurance Industry: An Interim Report*, Vol. II, *Minutes of Evidence and Appendices HC 272–II*. London: HMSO.

Select Committee on the Treasury (2001). *Sixth Report. HM Customs and Excise: Collection of Excise Duties* HC 237. London: HMSO.

Selznick, P. (1949). *TVA and the Grass Roots: A Study in the Sociology of Formal Organization.* Berkeley, CA: University of California Press.

Sheriff, P. (1976). 'The Sociology of Public Bureaucracies 1965–1975', *Current Sociology*, 24 (2): 1–175.

Sotiropoulos, D. (1999). 'A Description of the Greek Higher Civil Service', in E.C. Page and V. Wright (eds.), *Bureaucratic Elites in Western European States—A Comparative Analysis of Top Officials.* Oxford: Oxford University Press.

Sowa, J. E. and Selden, S. C. (2003). 'Administrative Discretion and Active Representation: An Expansion of the Theory of Representative Bureaucracy', *Public Administration Review*, 63(6): 700–10.

Steyn, J. (2001). 'Pepper v Hart. A Re-examination', *Oxford Journal of Legal Studies*, 21(1): 59–72.

Suleiman, E. N. (1978). *Elites in French Society.* Princeton, NJ: Princeton University Press.

Thain, C. (2002). 'The Core Executive Under Blair: The First Term', in S. Lancaster (ed.), *Developments in Politics 13.* Ormskirk: Causeway Press.

—— (2004). 'Treasury Rules OK? The Further Evolution of a British Institution', *British Journal of Politics and International Relations*, 6(1): 123–30.

—— and Wright, M. (1995). *The Treasury and Whitehall: The Planning and Control of Public Expenditure, 1976–1993*: Oxford: Clarendon Press.

Thatcher, M. and Stone Sweet, A. (eds.) (2002). 'The Politics of Delegation to Non-Majoritarian Institutions', Special Issue of *West European Politics*, 24(3).

Thoenig, J.-C. (1973). *L'Ere des technocrates—le cas des Ponts et Chaussées*: Paris: L'harmattan.

van Braam, A. (1957). *Ambtenaren en Bureaukratie in Nederland.* Zeist: Uitgeversmaatschappij W. de Haan N.V.

van der Meer, F. M. and Roborgh, L. J. (1993). *Ambtenaren in Nederland. Omvang, bureaucratisering en representativiteit van het ambtelijk apparaat.* Alphen aan den Rijn: Samsom H.D. Tjeenk Willink.

Weber, M. (1988). *Wirtschaft und Gesellschaft*, 5e. Auflage Tübingen: Mohr Siebeck.

Weiler, J. H. H. (1999). *The Constitution of Europe.* Cambridge: Cambridge University Press.

Wicks Committee (2003). *Defining the Boundaries within the Executive: Ministers, Special Advisers and the Permanent Civil Service*. London: Committee on Standards in Public Life (Wicks Committee), 9th Report, March.

Wilks, S. and Wright, M. (1987). 'Conclusion', in S.Wilks and M.Wright (eds.), *Comparative Government–Industry Relations*. Oxford: Clarendon Press.

Wilson, G. K. and Barker, A. (2003). 'Bureaucrats and Politicians in Britain', *Governance*, 16(3): 349–72.

Wilson, J. Q. (1989). *Bureaucracy: What Government Agencies Do and Why They Do It*. New York: Basic Books.

Wilson, R. (2001). Address by Sir Richard Wilson, Chartered Institute for Personnel and Development, Harrogate, 25 October 2001. London: Cabinet Office, available at http://www.cmps.gov.uk/speech.asp (accessed June 2004).

Wodehouse, P. G. (1923). *The Inimitable Jeeves*. London: Herbert Jenkins.

Wood, D. and Waterman, R. (1991). 'The Dynamics of Political Control of the Bureaucracy', *American Political Science Review*, 8(3): 801–28.

Worms, J. P. (1966). 'Le prefet et ses notables', *Sociologie de Travail*, 8: 249–75.

Wurzel, R. K. (1996). 'The Role of the EU Presidency in the Environmental Field: Does it Make a Difference Which Member State Runs the Presidency?', *Journal of European Public Policy*, 3(2): 272–91.

# Index